THE SILVER MADONNA

AND OTHER TALES OF AMERICA'S GREATEST LOST TREASURES

OTHER BOOKS BY W.C. JAMESON

Buried Treasures of America Series

Treasure Hunter: Caches, Curses, and Deadly Confrontations
Buried Treasures of the American Southwest
Buried Treasures of Texas
Buried Treasures of the Ozarks
Buried Treasures of the Appalachians
Buried Treasures of California
Buried Treasures of the Rocky Mountain West
Buried Treasures of the Great Plains
Buried Treasures of the South
Buried Treasures of the Pacific Northwest
Buried Treasures of New England
Buried Treasures of the Atlantic Coast
Buried Treasures of the Mid-Atlantic States
New Mexico Treasure Tales
Colorado Treasure Tales
Florida's Lost and Buried Treasures
Lost Mines and Buried Treasures of Arizona
Lost Mines and Buried Treasures of Old Wyoming
Lost Mines and Buried Treasures of Arkansas
Lost Mines and Buried Treasures of Missouri
Texas Tales of Lost Mines and Buried Treasures
Legend and Lore of the Guadalupe Mountains
Lost Mines and Buried Treasures of the Guadalupe Mountains
Lost Treasures in American History
Buried Treasures of the Ozarks and Appalachians
Finding Treasure: A Field Guide
Outlaw Treasures (audio)
Buried Treasures of the Civil War (audio)

Beyond the Grave Series

Butch Cassidy: Beyond the Grave

Billy the Kid: Beyond the Grave
John Wilkes Booth: Beyond the Grave

Books on Writing

Hot Coffee and Cold Truth: Living and Writing the West
Notes From Texas: On Writing in the Lone Star State
Want to be a Successful Writer? Do This Stuff
An Elevated View: Colorado Writers on Writing

Poetry

Bones of the Mountain
I Missed the Train to Little Rock
Open Range: Poetry of the Re-imagined West (edited with Laurie Wagner Buyer)

Food

Chili from the Southwest
The Ultimate Chili Cookbook

Fiction

Beating the Devil

Other

Unsolved Mysteries of the Old West
A Sense of Place: Essays on the Ozarks
Ozark Tales of Ghosts, Spirits, Hauntings, and Monsters

THE SILVER MADONNA

AND OTHER TALES OF AMERICA'S GREATEST LOST TREASURES

W.C. JAMESON

TAYLOR TRADE PUBLISHING
Lanham • New York • Boulder • Toronto • Plymouth, UK

Published by Taylor Trade Publishing
An imprint of The Rowman & Littlefield Publishing Group, Inc.
4501 Forbes Boulevard, Suite 200, Lanham, Maryland 20706
www.rowman.com

10 Thornbury Road, Plymouth PL6 7PP, United Kingdom

Distributed by National Book Network

British Library Cataloguing in Publication Information Available

Library of Congress Cataloging-in-Publication Data

Jameson, W. C., 1942–
  The Silver Madonna and Other Tales of America's Greatest Lost Treasures / W.C. Jameson.
    pages cm
  ISBN 978-1-58979-839-7 (pbk. : alk. paper) — ISBN 978-1-58979-840-3 (electronic) 1. Treasure troves—United States. I. Title.
  G525.J357 2013
  917.3—dc23
                                                              2013012809

∞™ The paper used in this publication meets the minimum requirements of American National Standard for Information Sciences—Permanence of Paper for Printed Library Materials, ANSI/NISO Z39.48-1992.

Printed in the United States of America

For Laurie

CONTENTS

THE SILVER MADONNA

AND OTHER TALES OF AMERICA'S GREATEST LOST TREASURES

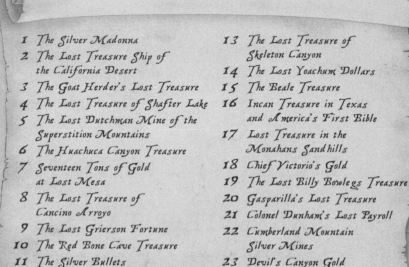

1 The Silver Madonna
2 The Lost Treasure Ship of
the California Desert
3 The Goat Herder's Lost Treasure
4 The Lost Treasure of Shafter Lake
5 The Lost Dutchman Mine of the
Superstition Mountains
6 The Huachuca Canyon Treasure
7 Seventeen Tons of Gold
at Lost Mesa
8 The Lost Treasure of
Cancino Arroyo
9 The Lost Grierson Fortune
10 The Red Bone Cave Treasure
11 The Silver Bullets
12 The Lost Gold Mine
of the Cossatot

13 The Lost Treasure of
Skeleton Canyon
14 The Lost Yoachum Dollars
15 The Beale Treasure
16 Incan Treasure in Texas
and America's First Bible
17 Lost Treasure in the
Monahans Sandhills
18 Chief Victorio's Gold
19 The Lost Billy Bowlegs Treasure
20 Gasparilla's Lost Treasure
21 Colonel Dunham's Lost Payroll
22 Cumberland Mountain
Silver Mines
23 Devil's Canyon Gold
24 The Incredible Journey of
the Confederate Treasury

PACIFIC
OCEAN

INTRODUCTION

The Silver Madonna, the inspiration for the title of this book, is a two-foot-tall statue fashioned from almost pure silver. It was stolen from a Canadian Indian village in 1759 and transported across the national border to a remote area in New Hampshire where it was lost. Its worth—both the silver and the historical—is inestimable. As a result of years of careful research, the location of this valuable object is likely known to within twenty feet. As you will discover, however, on reading about this and other lost treasures in this book, recovery sometimes offers greater challenges than discovery. As enhanced research opportunities and technology improve over time, however, the possibilities of locating and retrieving the Silver Madonna, as well as other treasures in this book, are growing.

For generations, Americans have thrilled at the prospect of mounting an expedition to go in search of some lost mine or buried treasure. Who has not longed to find a buried chest of gold coins, a cache of silver ingots, a stash of diamonds and emeralds? Who has never experienced the excitement of the quest for such things?

Tales of lost mines and buried treasures have captivated man's imagination since the dawn of civilization. A number of overland odysseys and dramatic sea voyages were initially undertaken as a search for riches of one kind or another. Many of the most popular myths and legends handed down over time from Greek, Roman, Scandinavian, and other cultures were about the quest for lost treasure. Dozens of the most enduring novels of the past decades deal with the search for lost and buried treasure: *Treasure Island*, *King Solomon's Mines*, and *Treasure*

1

of the Sierra Madre, to name a few. Contemporary author Clive Cussler's novels relating to searches for lost treasure hit the best-seller lists with each release. My own Buried Treasures of America series includes over thirty books that have enjoyed robust sales for over two decades. A memoir, *Treasure Hunter: Caches, Curses, and Deadly Confrontations*, was named Indie Reader Best Book of 2011.

Hollywood has long capitalized on the public's fascination with lost mines and buried treasures. Some of the most successful films in recent years include the Indiana Jones series, *National Treasure, Sahara, Fool's Gold*, and more. Additional films are being planned, as are a number of television series. There are five national magazines devoted specifically to treasure hunting.

Lost mines and buried treasures exist. I have made a career of searching for, locating, and writing about them. In recent years, significant discoveries have been reported: hundreds of millions of dollars in gold bullion from the sunken S.S. *Central America* off the Carolina coast; the discovery of thirty bars of buried gold ingots by an Arizona rancher; the amazing treasure recoveries from the Spanish vessel *Atocha* off the coast of Florida; 880 silver ingots found in a cave in the Mexican Sierra Madres.

For every lost treasure that is found, dozens, perhaps hundreds, more await discovery. Because of advances in detecting technology, research, and recovery techniques, more lost mines and buried treasures have been located in the past fifty years in the United States than ever before in history. The twenty-four tales included in this book are among the most famous and remain the most inviting to treasure hunters, professional and amateur. Not only are the stories compelling; the treasures themselves afford remarkable chances for discovery.

1

THE SILVER MADONNA

One of the greatest lost treasures in the history of the United States is a two-foot-tall statue crafted from what researchers maintain is pure silver. The figure, representing a mother and child, was called the Silver Madonna and was looted from a Canadian chapel in 1759 by a group of Robert Rogers' Rangers. While fleeing pursuit, the troopers carried the valuable idol to a location in New Hampshire where it was pushed into a river where, perhaps, it lies today. Between the silver content and the historical value, experts insist the Silver Madonna is worth several million dollars.

Captain Robert Rogers is identified in history books as the founder of Rogers' Rangers. The Rangers, initially composed of farmers, herders, and tradesmen from small New England villages, were brought together during the early 1750s by Rogers, who taught them the fundamental skills of fighting and warfare he had earlier learned from the Indians. He taught them how to track, the art of guerilla fighting, how to organize and conduct surprise raids, and how to endure a variety of adverse conditions. Rogers' Rangers served with the British Army during the French and Indian War (1754–1763) and were primarily responsible for scouting and conducting raids on enemy positions.

Though technically soldiers, the Rangers disdained rules, authority, and uniforms. They have been described as mercenaries, but some researchers regard the Rangers as little more than hired killers, in part because Rogers allowed his men to take scalps and loot villages and camps. Still others disagree and apply labels of "heroes" and "valuable assets" to the Rangers.

Rogers was born on November 7, 1731, in Methuen, Massachusetts. As a youth, he volunteered as a scout during conflicts between the settlers and Indians. From these same Indians, Rogers learned stealth, courage, camouflage, and survival techniques—skills that were to eventually serve him well during his period of leadership of the Rangers, the United States Army's first commandoes.

At the onset of the French and Indian War, the country of France, its Canadian colonies, and several allied American Indian tribes, waged war against Great Britain and the American colonies. The construction of Fort Duquesne by the French near the present-day city of Pittsburgh, Pennsylvania, is believed by most historians to have initiated the hostilities. The Virginia colony sent out a force to evict the French from the territory, at the time claimed by Virginia. The contingent was led by a twenty-two-year-old lieutenant named George Washington.

Major General William Shirley, realizing a need for the skills and services provided by Rogers' woods-wise and fearless fighting force, commissioned the group of sixty men in 1756. By July of 1758, Rogers was given the rank of major and the command of six hundred men.

During the war, relations between the French Canadians and the British and American colonies grew tense along the border between the two countries. Confrontations and conflict grew more frequent and violent, and General Jeffrey Amherst, commander of the British troops at Fort Ticonderoga, was becoming annoyed and concerned with the growing number of raids launched across the international border by the French and their Indian allies. Amherst knew of Rogers' Rangers and regarded them as an undisciplined and insubordinate gaggle of riff-raff. Furthermore, he despised Major Rogers.

In the final analysis, however, Amherst determined a retaliative strike across the Canadian border was in order and was well aware that his own troops were not up to the task and that no one, he was convinced, could carry it out but Rogers. The general met with Rogers and told him he wanted him to cross the border into Canada and launch a raid on an Abenaki Indian village known as St. Francis. Amherst instructed Rogers to give no quarter.

Twenty-two days following the meeting with Amherst, Rogers led a contingent of seven hundred Rangers to the outskirts of the Indian village in the middle of an October night in 1759. Thirty of his men were on horseback, the rest on foot. Packhorses transported supplies. After receiving a report from his scouts, Rogers issued instructions to his command. A short time later the Rangers had surrounded the village. Just as the rising sun illuminated the treetops of the adjacent forest, Rogers fired his musket, the signal to commence the assault.

The Rangers streamed into the village shooting and clubbing the surprised and confused Indians. Several were shot and killed as they slept on their pallets. Others were pulled from their shelters and executed on the spot. Women and children were slaughtered indiscriminately. A Catholic priest was dragged from the sanctuary of the chapel and killed.

So complete was the surprise attack that after only twenty minutes, more than two hundred Abenaki Indians lay dead in the village. The Indians' lodges were then set afire. While they blazed in the morning light, the Rangers went among the dead taking scalps and mutilating the corpses.

At this time, two dozen Rangers entered the chapel with the intention of sacking it. Golden candleholders, chalices, and crosses were snatched up and stuffed into canvas packs. On reaching the altar, a number of the Rangers halted and stared, stunned, at a remarkable statue perched on a wooden pedestal just behind it.

They had heard tales of this amazing statue but were not certain whether to believe them or not. It had been presented as a gift to the Abenakis a few years earlier. Just over two feet tall and crafted from native silver, a polished figure of a woman holding a child reflected the flickering light of the burning village. It was called the Silver Madonna. Once the initial surprise of encountering the statue had passed, several of the Rangers lifted it from the pedestal, carried it outside, and strapped it to the back of a packhorse.

Rogers surveyed the village to make certain that there were no survivors. This done, he assembled his troops and informed them that a handful of the Indians had escaped and would no doubt alert any French soldiers and other Indians nearby. He told them pursuit was imminent and that it was imperative they return immediately to Fort Ticonderoga.

With adrenalin still running high, Rogers' command set out, the officers mounted and the soldiers afoot. Supplies and munitions were reloaded onto the packhorses. The last two horses in the caravan carried the spoils taken from the chapel, including the Silver Madonna.

After two hours of brisk marching, a rear scout informed Rogers of a large force of armed and mounted French soldiers approaching rapidly from the direction of the village. Accompanying them, he said, were one hundred Indians. Realizing that his troops were growing exhausted from the long trek from Fort Ticonderoga, the battle, and the previous two hours of marching, Rogers considered that he needed an advantage. He split his force in order to confuse the pursuers. Rogers led one-half of the Rangers southward toward the border and the colonies. The remaining half was to leave the trail, enter the deep forest, and continue eastward for several miles before turning south. The packhorses carrying the loot from the chapel and the Silver Madonna followed the group that traveled to the east.

Rogers' attempt to confuse the pursuers was ineffective. On reaching the point in the trail where the force had separated, the French commanders wasted no time in dividing their own, sending one contingent to the south and the other to the east. Knowing they were closing in on the Americans, the French increased their pace in anticipation of overtaking them at any time. Only minutes later they caught up with both groups. Stragglers at the end of the fleeing columns were shot and killed, and the French soon closed in and engaged the remainder in hand-to-hand combat.

Finding themselves at a distinct disadvantage as a result of fatigue and surprise at the rapidity with which the French and Indians caught up with them, the Rangers suffered heavy casualties. The group fleeing toward the east suffered the most. Engaged in two full days of running and fighting with the French, they found no time to rest and eat. In addition, a severe snowstorm struck the region, which added to their hardship. Ill prepared to fight the French as well as protect themselves from the freezing temperatures, members of this Ranger party began deserting, fleeing southward through the woods in small groups at every opportunity.

The eastward-bound party of Rangers eventually arrived at the southwestern edge of Lake Memphremagog on the Vermont–Quebec border. The packhorse transporting the candlesticks, chalices, and other gold and silver church artifacts was tiring under the heavy weight.

Rather than take the time to cache the treasures, the Rangers simply abandoned them. They continued, however, to lead the packhorse carrying the Silver Madonna. Burdened by its load, the horse struggled, growing weaker with every mile. At one point where the lake was quite shallow, they decided to save time by crossing it. On reaching the opposite shore, the party, now much reduced in size as a result of desertion and death at the hands of their pursuers, turned southward and headed toward the Connecticut River. During their flight, the French and their Indian allies remained close behind, sometimes coming to within twenty yards of the Rangers, picking off a half-dozen of them each day.

The contingent of Rangers grew smaller, hungrier, more exhausted, and more desperate with each passing hour as they fled through the Vermont woods. By the time they reached the Connecticut River, only four of them survived, and they had run out of food. All they had in their possession were their guns and the packhorse carrying the Silver Madonna.

One of the Rangers, a sergeant named Amos Parsons, had some knowledge of the region through which they traveled and told his fellows that he was certain he could elude the pursuing French. After crossing the river and entering New Hampshire near the present day town of Lancaster, the exhausted Rangers followed the Israel River upstream and into the foothills of the White Mountains.

For two days they had experienced no pursuit. They assumed they had either eluded the French or, equally exhausted and out of provisions, their enemy simply turned back. For another two days, Parsons led his companions on a slow and difficult trek through the rugged foothills. The packhorse carrying the Silver Madonna had gone lame and had difficulty walking.

As wild game and berries were scarce to nonexistent because of the storm and the below-freezing weather, the soldiers were reduced to making soup out of strips of their buckskins. Weak and starved, they left the game trail that paralleled the river and ascended a narrow path with a number of switchbacks. After several minutes they found themselves in the shelter of an overhanging rock forty feet above the river. Here, they decided to stop and rest.

They unstrapped the Silver Madonna from the packhorse and carried it to the rear of the shelter. They then killed the animal, hacked off pieces of flesh with their hunting knives, and ate them raw. When their bellies were filled, they lay down on the floor of the shelter and slept for the first time in days.

Just before sunrise of the following morning, two of the Rangers awoke with severe stomach cramps. Parsons experienced a high fever accompanied by delirium. During one raging episode he became confused. He spotted the Silver Madonna at the rear of the shelter and crawled toward it. In his excited, manic stage, he reasoned that the idol was somehow responsible for all of the trials and troubles he and his companions had suffered. He pulled the statue from its hiding place, dragged it to the edge of the shelter, and pushed it over, letting it bounce and roll down the steep bank and into the Israel River. After watching the Madonna disappear beneath the waters of the stream, Parsons, now screaming and pulling clumps of hair from his head, dashed down the trail and into the woods. He was never seen again.

For another two days and nights, the three surviving Rangers lay in the rock shelter fighting their sickness and exhaustion. On the third morning, one of them awoke to find his companions had died during the night. Desperate, he fled from the shelter and resumed plodding up the trail that paralleled the Israel River. When darkness arrived, he sought shelter in a hollow log for the night. The following morning he rose and resumed his trek in hopes of encountering a farm or settlement where he might find help.

Around midmorning, the Ranger arrived at a small settlement of woodcutters consisting of five families. On spotting the pathetic, emaciated wretch wearing clothes that were little more than rags, the settlers took him in, fed him, and tried to make him comfortable.

Nearly two weeks passed before the Ranger was able to sit up and talk. He was lucid for only short periods at a time, but woke often during the night screaming and delirious. During his period of recovery, he told his caregivers about the Rangers' raid on the Abenaki village in Canada, the theft of the Silver Madonna, and the ordeal of fleeing from the French soldiers and Indians through the wilderness. In a very detailed narrative, he related how he and his companions lay in the rock shelter trying to recover from their illness and exhaustion. He told of how trooper Parsons pushed the Silver Madonna off the edge of the shelter and into the river.

With the passage of a few more days, the Ranger regained much of his health, but his mind never recovered from the ordeal. During his second month of living among the woodcutters he went completely insane.

On hearing the story of the Silver Madonna and its fate at the hands of trooper Parsons, one of the woodcutters said he knew the location of the rock shelter that was described by the Ranger. Two weeks later, he and three other men left the settlement one morning, followed the trail that paralleled the Israel River, and arrived at the specified location. They climbed the steep, switch-backing trail that led to the shelter and found the decayed remains of two men and a horse. They walked back and forth along the riverbank just below the shelter searching for some sign of the Silver Madonna, but the stream was too deep and swift at this location for them to spot anything. They returned to the settlement by dusk, empty-handed.

As far as anyone knows, the Silver Madonna has never been recovered, and most who have researched this tale are convinced it still lies at some location in the Israel River below the slope that leads to the rock shelter where the fleeing Rangers took refuge. Given an estimated weight of no less than one hundred and fifty pounds and the high specific gravity of silver, it is unlikely that the idol was carried downstream by the current for any significant distance from the point where it entered the river. As a result of several explorations into the region, there is reason to believe that the statue may have sunk a short distance into the soft mud of the bottom of the stream, or may have been covered over by gravel and silt carried by the river. The point where the Silver Madonna was pushed into the river is just downstream from the small New Hampshire settlement of Jefferson.

Today, the Silver Madonna is regarded as one of the most cherished artifacts from the French and Indian War. If recovered, the value of the silver at this writing is estimated to be around sixty to one hundred thousand dollars. The historical, antique, and collector value, however, would amount to several million dollars.

2

THE LOST TREASURE SHIP
OF THE CALIFORNIA DESERT

As unlikely as it seems, a seventeenth-century Spanish sailing vessel lies somewhere in the rugged, arid environment of the Southern California desert. Within the dune-covered hull of this ship that became stranded during a flood over four centuries ago lies a quantity of wooden casks, each filled to the top with rare black pearls harvested from the waters of the Gulf of California. Over the years and during the times the ship has been exposed by the constant winds, it has been encountered by travelers and prospectors but none were aware of its contents. Researchers estimate that if found today the cargo of pearls would be worth several million dollars.

In spite of the fact that the state of California is among the most populated in the United States, there exists a great swath in the extreme southern part that remains virtually uninhabited, a vast arid region that stretches from the Arizona border westward for over one hundred miles and southward into Mexico.

This expanse of sere landscape is called the Colorado Desert and is generally avoided by living things: human, plant, and animal. In response to the constant and high winds, the ever-shifting sands allow little opportunity for vegetation to take hold. Should a stray seed manage to find a place of refuge and germinate, the paucity of water in this area will keep it from reaching maturity. In addition to the lack of moisture and the extremely high temperatures, this land remains, for the most part, uninhabitable. Save for the occasional rattlesnake, scorpion, buzzard, or prospector, the region is seldom visited.

Hikers, explorers, and rock hounds visit the Colorado Desert of California from time to time to pit their skills against the elements, most of them perceiving the desert a worthy challenge. Many return to civilization, but a startling number of them succumb to dehydration, exposure, or snakebite. Indeed, during the history of this nation's westward expansion and settlement, Southern California's Colorado Desert has claimed the lives of hundreds.

Following the discovery of gold in California in 1849, along with the interest in seeking new environments in which to settle, practice agriculture, and establish businesses following the Civil War, tens of thousands of people migrated from the northern and eastern parts of the United States to California. A number of them, lured by the tales of opportunities to be found in and near the great cities and ports along Southern California's coast, elected to travel across this sere and forbidding landscape. Though warned of the dangers to be encountered in the Colorado Desert, many were convinced they would save time by selecting this route instead of traveling a safer road that circled many miles to the north.

Hundreds of the migrants selecting the more southern trace lost their lives, and for a time the desert floor was littered with the crosses of lonely graves along the way, markers that eventually succumbed to harsh desert winds and climate.

What may be even more remarkable, however, is that among those who managed to survive the perilous journey and reach the coast, there were some who related the strange tale of seeing an ancient masted sailing vessel partially buried in the sand dunes. On learning that the strange lost ship likely contained an uncountable fortune in exquisite pearls, some traveled back into the desert to search for it. Many were never seen again, and more returned with accounts of getting lost without food or water and not being able to relocate the ship.

In time, the complete story of the lost ship of the desert was revealed, causing hundreds more to enter the dunes to look for it. Some claimed to have found it but were never able to breach the protective cover of the desert sand. Others, travelers and prospectors, located it by accident over the years but were unaware of what was stored in the hold, only camped for the night and moved on.

Today, occasional reports of the lost treasure ship of the California desert continue to be received. Furthermore, it continues to be sought by professional treasure hunters as well as amateur searchers. At the end of the quest and deep inside the partially buried vessel are wooden casks of the rarest pearls in the history of the world.

✦

In the year 1610, Spain's King Philip III commanded Navy Captain Alvarez de Cordone to organize an expedition to search for pearls in Mexico's Gulf of California, located between the west coast and the elongated peninsula of Baja California. During previous expeditions to the area, the Spanish learned that a rare large mollusk made its home in the shallow water along the coast and produced an exceptional pearl with a dark, nearly black, shiny, metallic surface. The Spanish explorers discovered that the local Indians harvested these fine pearls from the waters and used them to fashion necklaces and other jewelry. During this time, pearls were considered more valuable than gold. In addition to adding to the wealth of the Spanish treasury, King Philip knew well that the country's upper class, as well as that of other European royalty, coveted the rare gems, and he wished to control the market for them.

At the time, Captain Cordone was headquartered in Mexico City. He was known to be intensely loyal to the government of Spain and to King Philip in particular. As was Spanish custom, the commander of an expedition sent to recover gold, silver, or any other kind of wealth received a generous share. Cordone entertained visions of becoming a wealthy man as well as a member of an elite Spanish society. He further imagined he would be rewarded with higher rank and perhaps an important political appointment. Cordone was anxious to carry out King Philip's orders.

According to his instructions, Cordone was to oversee the design and construction of three ships. He was provided free rein relative to the organization and outfitting of the vessels in order to ensure the success of the expedition. Wasting little time, Cordone ordered the reassignment of two respected and trusted officers to assist him—Captains Juan de Iturbe and Pedro de Rosales. The three men, accompanied by an armed escort, traveled 250 miles south to the coastal city of Acapulco, where they supervised the construction of the ships and pursued preparations for the voyage. While work progressed on the vessels, Cordone requested sixty experienced pearl divers be recruited from the east coast of Africa and shipped to Acapulco.

The ships were finally completed during July 1612. Following two weeks of trials to test their seaworthiness, Cordone announced he was ready to lead the expedition. A few days later, he ordered the three ships into the blue waters of the Pacific Ocean and along a northwesterly course that paralleled Mexico's shore.

As the three Spanish ships sailed through the calm coastal waters, occasional anchorings were ordered so that the divers could explore the rocky bottoms for promising oyster beds. Now and then some pearls were harvested, but Cordone knew from previous reports that the richest beds lay farther to the north and deeper into the Gulf of California. It was to this region he guided the expedition.

After several weeks of sailing, one of Cordone's lookouts spotted an Indian village on a nearby shore. After observing the natives for a time, Cordone noted that the males appeared to be diving for pearls in the shallow waters. Considering that he might find a store of pearls among these indigenes, Cordone ordered the anchors dropped. The captain, accompanied by a contingent of crewmen as well as some soldiers in case of a hostile reception, landed ashore and requested to speak with the village headman.

According to the chief, Cordone and his men were the first Europeans to visit the village. To Cordone's delight, the Indians proved to be friendly and the reception was warm. Communicating in signs, the chief invited the Spaniards to share the evening meal with the small tribe. Long into the night Cordone and the chief conversed about a variety of topics. By the time the sun rose, Cordone determined it was time to inquire about the pearls being harvested from the sea floor.

The chief told the Spaniard that the shellfish were harvested primarily for food and from time to time a pearl would be found. When this occurred, it was removed and stored with others that had accumulated. When one of the tribe wished to make a necklace or some other item of jewelry, they simply went to where the pearls were stored and retrieved any amount necessary. When Cordone asked if he could see the pearls, the chief escorted him to a nearby shelter and pointed to two clay pots, each filled to the top with black pearls. Cordone estimated it was a fortune large enough to satisfy a dozen kings.

When Cordone asked the chief if he would like to trade for some of the pearls, the Indian expressed interest in the clothes worn by the Spaniards. He told Cordone that he and members of his tribe would indeed look splendid garbed in such finery as that manifested by the officers and soldiers. Following several minutes of bartering the two men settled on an agreement and Cordone, along with his escort, returned to the ship.

The following morning, several bundles of clothing, neatly folded and tied, were loaded into a rowboat and transported to the shore by a handful of crewmen. Awaiting them were the chief and a half-dozen members of the tribe standing next to the two clay pots filled with pearls. After unloading the bundles of clothing, the crewmen placed the heavy pots into the boat and rowed back toward the ship. As the crewmen steered the rowboat toward the ships, the Indians opened the bundles and were surprised that they contained not the fine clothes worn by the Spanish officers and soldiers, but a motley collection of rags and discarded garments.

Screaming angry insults at the departing Spaniards, several of the Indians waded knee-deep into the water and loosed arrows toward the rowboat. Others, brandishing spears and bows and arrows, piled into nearby log canoes and made for the three ships.

On reaching the closest vessel, one commanded by Iturbe, the crewmen in the rowboat quickly loaded the pearls and scrambled aboard. Following shouted commands by Cordone, anchors were raised, sails were hoisted, and the vessels were soon under way. For several minutes, the canoes of the Indians kept pace with the departing ships. Now and then crewmen would dodge an arrow that was fired onto the decks.

Cordone, delighted with himself for swindling the gullible Indians out of a fortune in pearls, stood at the railing of his ship smiling down at the pursuers. He was about to order his soldiers to fire upon the Indians when he was struck in the chest by an arrow. He dropped to the deck.

The next day, Cordone, attended by the ship's surgeon, suffered a high fever and experienced great pain. The surgeon suspected blood poisoning and recommended returning to Acapulco where the captain could be more effectively treated. Otherwise, said the doctor, Cordone would surely die.

At first, Cordone dismissed the diagnosis as an overreaction on the part of the surgeon, but eventually he accepted it. He instructed Iturbe and Rosales to continue up the coast into the Gulf of California in the remaining two ships and harvest more pearls. In the far northern reaches of the gulf, Cordone was convinced, lay the richest oyster beds.

Several days later, the ships commanded by Iturbe and Rosales entered the Gulf of California. True to Cordone's prediction, they encountered a number of rich mollusk beds that yielded great quantities of the dark, gleaming pearls that were stored in the wooden kegs brought along for the specific purpose of transporting the fortune. As the black divers harvested the floor of the sea, the two captains determined to sail as far north as possible in hopes of finding more and larger oyster beds. The two officers, like Cordone, were convinced that if they returned to Mexico City with a great fortune in pearls, they would be rewarded with promotions and influential assignments. Their swelling lust for power and status was to prove their undoing.

Captain Iturbe agreed with Cordone that the richest oyster beds were to be found at the extreme northern part of the gulf where it receives the nutrient rich outflow of the Colorado River, and it was to this location the ships were directed. The ship under the command of Captain de Rosales rode quite low in the water as a result of the great weight of pearls it transported. One afternoon as the two ships sailed northward in the placid waters just off the coast of a small island named Isla Angel de Guardia, de Rosales's vessel struck a reef and suffered a tear in the wooden hull. As the ship sank into the sea, crewmen worked frantically to transfer its cargo of pearls onto Iturbe's vessel.

Moments after the final keg was loaded onto the ship, de Rosales's boat slipped below the surface and settled onto the bottom sands several fathoms below. The cargo hold of the remaining ship was completely filled with casks of pearls and twice the normal contingent of crewmen and now it, too, floated dangerously low in the waters. In spite of this, the two officers determined to continue sailing northward in search of even more oyster beds and, they dreamed, greater wealth for the country of Spain and themselves.

Several more days passed, and finally Iturbe's ship, aided by strong southerly winds, sailed into the estuarine waters where the Colorado River entered the gulf. During that time this river, unencumbered by the dams that regulate flow today, carried a much greater load of water. According to geologists, during periods of increased drainage, it was not unusual for the Colorado River to overflow its banks and contribute to the formation of large inland bodies of water such as the Salton Sea, a remnant of which is still found in Southern California. The geologists further explain that earthquakes, which are common in the region, can cause significant changes in the topography. The San Andreas Fault, one that is quite active, lies just beneath the sands of Southern California's Colorado Desert. During a major quake, which occurred a short time prior to Iturbe's visit, the channel of the Colorado River was shifted eastward as much as fifty or more miles to its present location, leaving behind a landlocked body of water.

Additionally, at a location some sixty miles upstream from where Iturbe entered, the river had broken through a section of its bank and spilled out of its channel into the low-lying area to the west and created a large inland sea. Although the river was shallow, it carried just enough water to accommodate the heavily laden ship. Days later, Iturbe's vessel left the river and sailed into the inland sea. Still obsessed with finding pearls, Iturbe and de Rosales instructed the divers to search for more oyster beds.

For two weeks, the Spaniards sailed around this sea before it dawned on them that it was only a shallow accumulation outflow from the river and would hold no oyster beds. Iturbe issued the order to return to the channel and thence back to the waters of the Gulf of California. As they neared the channel, however, they discovered that as a result of a drop in the water level, a low ridge of land separated the sea from the river. The Spaniards were horrified to realize they were now landlocked with no chance of returning to the gulf.

Hopeful that he might be able to locate another route to the open sea, Iturbe sailed once again around the shallow sea only to return to the same location days later. He realized that not only was the ship trapped with no hope of escaping this watery realm, but the intense evaporation generated by the high temperatures was causing the level to lower at a rapid rate. While pursuing yet another search for a route to the gulf, the Spanish vessel came to rest on the sandy bottom of the lake. As days passed and the water continued to recede, the ship began listing to one side.

As the hopelessness of the situation was realized, the two captains, the crew, the divers, and the soldiers gathered up what provisions they could carry, abandoned the stranded ship, and struck out across the drying lake bed toward the Gulf of Mexico. As they traveled southward, Iturbe and de Rosales cast glances back toward the vessel, each one thinking about the fortune in black pearls stored in casks and strapped into the hold.

Four months later, the survivors reached a location along the western coast of Mexico near the present-day city of Guaymas, where they were spotted by a lookout on a Spanish galleon. They were rescued and transported to Acapulco, and thence to Mexico City. Less than half of those who had set out from the stranded vessel survived the journey. The rest succumbed to thirst, starvation, exposure, Indian attacks, and snakebite.

As the members of the pearl gathering expedition were being carried back to Acapulco, Iturbe's ship came to rest at a forty-five degree angle on the now dry floor of the desert. By this time, the relentless winds had rendered the canvas sail to tatters and piled the drifting sands deep along the windward side of the vessel, accumulating nearly to the gunwales. Deep within the hold, an uncountable fortune in pearls reposed in several wooden casks and two clay pots, all covered with an accumulating layer of dust. For more than two centuries, the treasure-filled vessel lay thus before it was looked upon by another human being. Sometimes it was hidden by the ever-shifting sands, other times it lay partially exposed.

In time, the survivors of the disastrous pearl hunting expedition were returned to Mexico City where Captain Iturbe submitted a report of what had transpired. The document was examined by an official or two, and then filed away. It was determined that the shortage of manpower and the expense of mounting a recovery expedition were too great to consider.

It was over two centuries later that the remarkable story of the stranded Spanish ship with its cargo of pearls lost somewhere in the desert of Southern California became known. As a result, dozens of expeditions entered the arid and forbidding region between the Colorado River and the Vallecito Mountains in search of the vessel. In spite of the numerous quests, several of them well-funded, the ship could not be found. On returning, some claimed that the ship was more than likely buried under several feet of drifting sand. Others advanced the notion that it never existed.

During the years following the Civil War, hundreds of migrants desirous of finding a short route to the California coast, attempted the trek across the arid expanse of the Colorado Desert. Dozens lost their lives. Like the travelers before them, some who managed to reach Los Angeles or San Diego told of having spotted the remains of an old and weathered sailing ship out in the middle of this vast arid region.

During the 1880s, lured by the chance of finding gold and other precious metals, prospectors entered this desert to search for signs of ore in the rock outcrops that dotted the environment. On returning to nearby settlements for supplies, some of these prospectors reported spotting the remains of a ship half-buried in the sand at some remote location. Most were unaware of the cargo contained within the ship's hold. Others told of running low on water or food and were unable to investigate the ship further.

One long-time prospector told of spending most of a year in the area searching for signs of ore in the nearby exposed granite and camping in the lee of the old vessel. He described the weathered and rotted wood of the ship, some of which he used for his campfires. When told the story of the ship's cargo of pearls, he determined to return to the location and retrieve it. In spite of repeated attempts, he was never able to find the ship again.

In 1882, a group of prospectors were on their way to examine some outcrops near Superstition Mountain, located in present-day Imperial County and thirty miles northwest of the border town of Calexico and just south of the Salton Sea. Along the way, they encountered a long pole lying partially buried in the desert sand. One of the members of the party identified the object as the mast of a ship. Another recalled the tale of the lost treasure ship allegedly stranded somewhere in this desert. For the next several days, the prospectors searched the region for the ship but found nothing. They finally determined it was buried under one of the high dunes in the area.

In 1915, an old man, a Yuma Indian, walked into the desert town of Indio. After entering a small grocery store and selecting some items, he attempted to pay for them with a handful of small, round, black stones. As he was discussing the exchange, the proprietor of the store realized the stones were, in fact, pearls. On inquiring about the source of the stones, the Indian told of becoming lost as he was traveling across the desert and seeking shelter in what he described as a large "wooden house" almost entirely covered in sand. Inside this house, he explained, he encountered several wooden barrels, each filled to the top with the stones.

Before the day was over, the story told by the Indian was being related all over town. A group of men approached the Indian and offered him two hundred dollars in cash if he would lead them to the "wooden house." The Indian agreed and was paid the money and given a place to spend the night. In the morning, however, he could not be found and was never seen again.

As recently as 2004, hikers, trail bikers, and some rock hounds and meteorite hunters have returned from the deep interior of California's Colorado Desert with reports of encountering the bow or stern of an old ship partially buried in the sand. None were aware of the story of Captain Iturbe's lost treasure ship. On learning the story, some attempted to relocate the vessel but were never successful.

Given the continuous shifting of the desert sands as a result of the strong and constant winds found here, it remains likely that the lost Spanish treasure ship is alternately covered and exposed. Some day when a portion of the vessel is exposed, some hiker or trail biker may chance upon it and discover the fortune outlined in black pearls lying within.

From time to time, a satellite image encountered on the Google Earth Internet site shows promise. In 2009, one such image depicted what appeared to be the outline of a portion of what looks similar to that of a sailing ship at a location not far from Superstition Mountain. Months later when a small expedition arrived at the site, nothing was found save for an expanse of rippling dunes. The leader of the expedition suspected the object of their search had been covered over by the blowing sand.

The quest to find the lost treasure-laden Spanish ship in the Colorado Desert continues.

3

THE GOAT HERDER'S
LOST TREASURE

One of the most fascinating and compelling lost treasures in America is one that was found by a simple, uncomplicated man who was frightened by it. After informing others of his discovery, he feared the consequences and fled, never to return. For more than half a century, this treasure has attracted dozens of searchers. It has been found on two occasions, and then lost again both times.

✦

The Guadalupe Mountains of West Texas are notable for a number of reasons. For one, the range houses Guadalupe Peak, the highest point in Texas at 8,751 feet. For another, the mountains were the last stronghold for the Mescalero Apaches. For yet another, the Guadalupe Mountains may be the site for more lost mines and buried treasures than any other geographic location in America.

One such tale involves an amazing discovery of chests filled with gold and silver coins that were found in a remote cave by a goat herder. The discovery was to change his life, and the search for this fortune continues.

Before white settlers arrived in the region of the Guadalupe Mountains, the grasses native to the area were plentiful and rich in nutrients. Because of this, the newcomers saw great potential in the region for grazing livestock. Before long, several cattle, sheep, and goat raising enterprises were operating on and along the flanks of these mountains.

During the early part of the twentieth century, a man named J. C. Hunter envisioned the front range of the Guadalupe Mountains as having great potential for raising Angora goats. At the time, the demand for mohair, the yarn made from the silky hair of this goat, was great and those who could keep the eastern markets supplied with it were making good profits. Hunter was convinced he could make a fortune with a successful Angora ranching operation in the range. History proved him correct.

Before much time passed, Hunter moved large herds of Angora goats onto his property on which he also grazed cattle and sheep. Hunter employed a number of cowhands and goat and sheep herders. One of his goat herders was a young man named Jesse Duran.

Duran, along with his parents, had migrated from the interior of Mexico and crossed the Rio Grande into Texas, coming north in search of work on one of the prosperous ranches. A skilled herder in his native Mexico, Duran soon found employment on the Hunter Ranch and was placed in charge of a large herd of goats that grazed the eastern limits of the ranch along the slopes and foothills.

Jesse Duran was a simple, uncomplicated young man. He never owned anything of value during his lifetime. With his job on the Hunter Ranch, his basic needs for food and shelter were met. He longed for little else. Though he received a small salary, Duran had little need for money, and sent his earnings to his parents, who chose to live and work in Laredo.

Duran was with his herd one misty spring morning in 1930 when he noticed his canteen was empty. The goats were grazing contentedly among the sparse vegetation atop Rader Ridge, a low, narrow limestone crest that extends out from the southeastern escarpment of the Guadalupe Mountains and extends toward the El Paso–Carlsbad road two miles away. It had been raining for two days, a cold rain accompanied by a brisk wind. Duran, wrapped in a worn woolen poncho, watched the goats from the shelter of a madrone tree. Presently, he decided to walk over to nearby Juniper Spring to fill his canteen.

Juniper Spring lay a mile to the southwest and downhill from where Duran sat. He turned into the wind and struck out for the spring. After a few minutes of hiking the narrow goat trail, Duran attempted a shortcut across a gently sloping limestone outcrop. The route would shorten his walk, but it proved to be considerably rougher than the trail. Large slabs of weathered rock lay everywhere, and Duran walked around on top of many of them. Once, as he stepped onto a rain-slicked slab of stone it gave way under him and slid downslope, spilling the goat herder to the ground. When Duran rose and wiped the mud and desert debris from his pants and poncho, he noticed a small opening in the outcrop where the large flat stone had earlier rested.

In the dim light of the cloudy morning, Duran peered into a low, shallow cave. As his eyes became accustomed to the dark interior, Duran recoiled from what he saw. Just inside the opening and propped up against one wall of the cave were three skeletons with what was left of their clothes hanging loosely from their bones. Leaning against the opposite wall of the cave were at least three rifles.

Then Duran saw something else. Lying on the floor of the cavern just beyond the skeletons were three strongboxes of the type used by Wells Fargo and the Butterfield Overland Mail to transport money and gold. One of the boxes was open, and it was filled with gold and silver coins. Duran touched nothing in the cave. He refused to enter or even extend his head in beyond the opening. Frightened, he replaced the stone slab over the opening. He continued on to Juniper Spring to fill his canteen and pondered what to do with his discovery.

Later that afternoon, Duran decided to tell the ranch foreman what he found. Making certain that his goats were secure, he walked several miles to the home of Frank Stogden, arriving at his house one hour past sundown. After knocking on the back door, Duran was greeted by Stogden's wife. She invited him in out of the rain and offered him some coffee. She told Duran that her husband and three neighboring ranchers were playing cards in another room and that he would see him as soon as they were finished.

An hour later, Stogden called Duran into the room. He and the other men listened to the goat herder's description of his amazing discovery. Stogden and his friends told Duran they would be ready to ride out at first light and recover the treasure, but the herder was hesitant. He explained to the men that he feared the spirits of the dead that he believed inhabited the cave and watched over all that was inside it. Duran was a devout Catholic with a strong belief in the power of departed souls. He explained that any treasure found with skeletons was destined to remain where it was, and that any who disturbed the site would bring bad luck and hardship, perhaps even death, to themselves and their families. Duran said he believed nothing but evil could come from desecrating the treasure cave.

The ranchers laughed at Duran's fear and said that spirits did not intimidate them. Then they pressed Duran for directions to the cave. Their eagerness made Duran cautious, and as he grew more nervous, the ranchers backed off of their insistence, not wanting to risk continued refusal. The men told Duran they would turn in for the night and continue discussion of the treasure cave in the morning, then ride out to Rader Ridge and examine it. The next morning, however, Duran was gone. He was never seen in the vicinity of the Guadalupe Mountains again.

In the morning, Stogden and the three other men saddled their horses and rode to Rader Ridge, arriving at Juniper Spring just before noon. The continuing rain had obliterated any sign of Duran's presence in the area. The men dismounted, hitched their horses to bushes, and began searching the rugged area on foot.

According to Duran's story, as it was recounted by these same men years later, the young goat herder found the small cave while making his way downslope from the top of Rader Ridge. Leaving the narrow trail, Duran walked several more yards along a limestone outcrop before slipping on the flat rock. Jesse had told the men that as he stood at the opening of the treasure cave he was about one-quarter mile northeast of Juniper Spring.

The four ranchers searched until sundown but found nothing. On several occasions they encountered large flat slabs of rock, but when they shifted them aside there was no cave beneath any of them. For several months, the four men returned to the area to search for the cave when their responsibilities permitted, but having no luck they eventually gave up the search.

As time passed, others heard the story of Jesse Duran's treasure cave, and soon the hills between Rader Ridge and Juniper Spring were covered with treasure hunters. In spite of all efforts to locate the treasure, however, the mysterious cave still remains hidden somewhere on the rocky slope of the mountain.

Continued research into the story told by Jesse Duran supports the notion that the treasure cave does indeed exist and in all probability contains a fortune in gold and silver coins as well as skeletons and rifles.

The Guadalupe Mountains are a massive limestone reef transecting the Texas–New Mexico border and extending for nearly two hundred miles. The range is pockmarked with hundreds of caves, large and small. A half-hour drive toward the northeast along State Highway 62-180 would bring one to Carlsbad Caverns. Lechuguilla Cave, regarded as the largest cave system in the world, is also located in this mountain range. Within a half-mile of Juniper Spring are several small caves similar to the one described by Duran.

The Butterfield stage line passed less than one mile from Juniper Spring, and the Pinery, a stage stop for the Butterfield Overland Mail, had been constructed at the top of the pass. The rock building and its associated corrals was a location where horses, weary from the long pull up the mountain, were exchanged for fresh ones and where passengers could enjoy a meal and a bed. During its brief existence, the Butterfield Overland Mail transported money, supplies, and passengers from the east to the newly settled land and associated business opportunities in the west. From Arizona, California, and New Mexico, the line transported shipments of gold and money from the mines there to the eastern banks.

It is also a fact that bandits hid out in the deep and forbidding canyons of the Guadalupe Mountains. Outlaws preyed on the stage-coaches as the horses labored up the steep grades toward the Pinery Station. Records show that stages were halted, passengers robbed, and strongboxes and chests containing gold, money, and ore were taken on several occasions.

Given these facts, it is not unreasonable to conclude that the cave Jesse Duran found was a cache for goods taken from the stage line. More difficult to explain is the presence of the three skeletons in the cave. Perhaps they were victims of the robbers. Or maybe there was a falling out among the bandits and three of their number were slain and left in the cave.

Elsewhere in the Guadalupe range other strongboxes and chests have been found and documented. In some cases it has been suggested that the principals involved in the robberies were captured or killed by pursuing lawmen and never had an opportunity to return to retrieve their booty.

Duran himself is a fundamental element pertinent to the credibility of this tale of lost treasure. Old-timers in the region who knew Duran claimed that he was an honest, sincere, trustworthy, practical, and hard-working young man not given to exaggeration or making up stories. Duran was well liked and had the respect of all who knew him.

In researching Duran, it was learned that, following his visit with Stogden and his neighbors, the goat herder fled on foot that same night to Carlsbad, New Mexico, some seventy-five miles to the northeast. He went directly to the home of a sister where he related his experience. Duran remained hidden at the sister's place for three months, rarely leaving the house during daylight hours.

Duran's fear of the spirits of the dead was so strong that he continued to believe his accidental discovery of the treasure and the skeletons might bring bad luck to his family. So greatly did he fear the situation that he decided to leave his sister's home and travel to California. There, Duran worked as a farm laborer until the day he died sometime in the early 1970s.

Evidence exists that others may have stumbled onto Jesse Duran's treasure cave. Sam Hughes operated a successful cattle and sheep ranch in Dog Canyon on a northern portion of the Guadalupe range. One day, Hughes, along with several friends, was deer hunting near Juniper Spring when he accidentally slipped into the opening of a small cave. Afraid there might be rattlesnakes lurking inside, Hughes immediately extricated himself and continued on with his hunt. At the time, Hughes was unaware of the tale of Jesse Duran's treasure cave.

Later that evening as Hughes and his companions were relating the day's activities around the campfire, the rancher told his story of falling into the shallow cave. Noel Kincaid, who at the time was foreman of the J. C. Hunter Ranch and occasional searcher for the treasure cave, asked Hughes for more details. His description of the cave matched that of Duran's. It was also about one-quarter mile northeast of Juniper

Spring. The following morning, the deer hunters set out to try to relocate the cave but had no luck.

During the 1950s and 1960s, a man named Lester White camped in and explored around the Guadalupe Mountains. He was a white-bearded, sun-wrinkled outdoorsman who spent much of his time searching throughout the range for lost mines and buried treasures. A throwback to the old-time prospectors and miners of a bygone era, White differed only in that instead of a pack mule he negotiated his way around the flanks of the range in an old pickup truck. He made camp wherever he wound up at the end of the day. He had spent fifteen years in the Guadalupe Mountains but was unacquainted with the tale of Jesse Duran's treasure cave.

Sometimes while visiting with others in the area, White would relate an experience about finding a small cave in the exposed bedrock about one mile northeast of the old Frijole ranch house and not too far from Juniper Spring. He found the cave by accident, he said, while he was resting one evening near an old goat trail that led up to Rader Ridge. He explained that, just below where he sat, odd shadows cast by the setting sun from a large and flat limestone rock suggested a hole immediately adjacent to it. Making his way down the slope toward the rock, White noted that the rock had apparently slid several inches down the slope, revealing the opening to a small cave.

White, a thin, rather frail man, was unable to budge the rock any further. He peered into the small opening next to the rock. What he saw, he stated, caused the hair on the back of his neck to stiffen. Inside the cave, he said, "was at least two skeletons and a bunch of old rotted clothes and boots." White claimed he had found skeletons in the range before and was not particularly interested in any of them. He turned from the cave and made his way back to his camp.

Others have reported encountering this elusive little cave in the past but, not knowing what lay inside, never ventured beyond the opening for fear of snakes or for lack of interest. Large flat limestone slabs of rock lie everywhere in this portion of the range, and checking under each of them would be a formidable task. All it takes is shifting the right one to the side, however, to reveal the opening to a small cave that holds riches that have eluded searchers for over a century.

4

THE LOST TREASURE
OF SHAFTER LAKE

Most Americans are familiar with some of the more well-known tales of lost and buried treasure in the West such as the gold of Arizona's Superstition Mountains and the Lost Sublette Mine of Texas's Guadalupe Mountains. Only a handful, however, are aware of an incredible fortune in gold, large enough to require two mule-drawn wagons to transport, that lies beneath the surface of a dry lake bed on the High Plains of Texas. According to researchers, this mysterious and elusive treasure may be worth in excess of twenty million dollars today.

$$\oplus$$

Following the end of the War Between the States, a number of Union army officers were assigned duty in the expanding frontier of the United States. New settlers were flocking into the West at an increasing rate, seeking to undertake farming, ranching, and mining, and establish towns with schools, churches, and businesses.

Difficulty arose when the land sought by these newcomers was the homelands of dozens of different tribes of American Indians. In seeking to defend their traditional ranges, the Indians waged war on the settlers, and the results were often bloody. Soon, the growing demands for protection were heeded by the U.S. government. Military forts and outposts were established and fortified with contingents of soldiers who patrolled vast areas in an attempt to bring order and peace.

William Rufus Shafter enlisted in the army of the North soon after the outbreak of the Civil War. By the time he reached his twenty-sixth birthday, he had accumulated battle experience at Ball's Bluff, Fair Oaks, Nashville, Yorktown, and West Point. A fearless fighter, Shafter was often wounded, twice decorated, and won the praise and admiration of General George Henry Thomas, known to his troops as the Rock of Chickamauga. In recognition for Shafter's achievements during the war, Thomas presented him the command of a large contingent of black soldiers, called Buffalo Soldiers by the Indians, assigned to frontier Texas. Shortly after arriving at his post, Shafter earned a reputation as a courageous and indomitable leader who rode into battle without hesitation and won the respect of his troops. During Shafter's time in West Texas, he earned the nickname "Pecos Bill."

In 1957, a researcher examining a collection of military documents from the 1860s and 1870s located in a Fort Bliss, Texas, depository, encountered a cryptic report pertaining to Shafter and a contingent of soldiers escorting two wagonloads of gold from the Mexican border to some unidentified destination in the north. The source of the gold was not indicated and remains a mystery to this day. In addition, it was not specified whether the gold was in the form of ore, ingots, or coins, and an estimate of value was never recorded. It must be assumed, however, that "two wagonloads of gold" represented a substantial fortune.

The paucity of information regarding the gold shipment has led to the suggestion by some that Pecos Bill Shafter may have acquired it illegally and intended it for his own use. Shafter supporters have taken issue with this view and resent what they consider to be a slur upon the officer's character. In response, they offered the explanation that it was more likely he was on a secret mission for the U.S. government and that the gold was being transported to the U.S. Treasury in Denver.

Whatever the truth of the matter, the gold never reached its intended destination and lies today beneath the bottom of a dry lake bed in Andrews County on the High Plains of West Texas, a shallow playa called Shafter Lake.

Located a few miles northwest of the city of Andrews, Texas, Shafter Lake is not so much a true lake as it is a mostly dry but occasionally water-filled depression in the arid, semidesert environment. Hundreds of such depressions dot the Texas Panhandle and vary in size. Many are little more than ponds, but a few of the larger ones are regarded as legitimate lakes by the area residents. They are sometimes filled with saline-laden waters from runoff generated by the infrequent thunderstorms that visit this part of the country. The often intense heat of the region, coupled with the low relative humidity, facilitates rapid evaporation of the playa waters, leaving behind crusty accumulations of salt. Shafter Lake is one such playa and remains dry much of the year, often for several years in a row.

Shafter, leading his contingent of mounted troopers and the two mule-drawn wagonloads of gold, had passed two miles east of the small town of Monahans and was traveling in a northeasterly direction when one of his scouts informed him that a band of forty Comanches was following a short distance behind. Well aware of the danger represented by these Indians, Shafter ordered six sharpshooters to the rear of the small caravan. Their presence, he hoped, would deter any attack planned by the raiders.

Throughout the day, the Comanches remained a mile behind the soldiers, never advancing or making overt threats. A few minutes before sundown, the soldiers arrived at a small spring located not far from the present-day town of Notrees, twenty-five miles north of Monahans. Here, Shafter ordered a halt, instructed the men to set up camp, and posted a double guard around the perimeter. Few of the soldiers slept that night as they peered into the darkness looking for any sign of the Comanches they knew were just a short distance away.

The troopers were up before dawn the following day, and after a hasty, cold breakfast, continued on the trail northward once again. As the rising sun illuminated the flat plains, the soldiers could see the Comanches about a mile to the south, still following.

Travel was slow owing to the sand-choked trails and occasional deep washes and gullies across which they had to negotiate the heavily laden wagons. Three more days passed, and the party finally made camp one evening a short distance from the southwestern shore of a large playa.

Several soldiers hauled water barrels out to the shallow lake to replenish what had been used but found it too salty to drink. They contented themselves with a bath, the first they'd had in several days, and noted that the lake was only two to three feet deep.

That evening as Shafter and his soldiers ate supper, one of the lieutenants, who had been studying the lake, decided they would make better time by traveling across the lake rather than around it. Though he had not investigated, he insisted the lake bottom was firm enough to support the wagons, mules, and horses.

The next morning, the troopers dined once again on a cold breakfast, hitched the mule teams to the wagons, and mounted up. Moments later, Shafter motioned the contingent forward and into the playa, his intention being to avoid the long route around the body of water.

Initially, the crossing was uneventful. The saline waters of the playa lapped at the boots of the riders and the wagon bottoms, but progress was no slower than what they had grown accustomed to. As the party neared the middle of the lake, however, trouble started. The lead pair of mules became bogged in the soft mud and was unable to proceed. As the soldiers worked to free them, the trailing pair began sinking, soon followed by the wagon itself. Within ten minutes, the first wagon had vanished below the surface of the water and the second one, along with its mule team, was slowly disappearing into the saturated sands and silts in the bottom of the lake. Extra horses and mules were brought in and harnessed to the wagons and mules, but to no avail. They, too, sank into the mud and drowned.

As Shafter watched the futile efforts to save the wagons and the gold, the Comanches arrived at the south end of the lake. Forming a single line stretched out along the shore, they remained mounted while observing the frantic activities of the troopers. When it became clear that the quarry was in a somewhat defenseless position, the leader of the Comanches issued a loud cry and sent his armed warriors into the lake toward the confused soldiers. After regarding the approaching Comanches for a moment, Shafter ordered his disorganized men to mount up, abandon the wagons, and ride away. When they reached the north shore, they did not stop, but continued their flight from the pursuing Indians across the dry plains.

The Indians chased the soldiers for four miles before reining up. Returning to the mired wagons and animals in the middle of the lake, they found little useful save for some harnesses, ropes, and sheets of canvas. Careful to avoid being trapped in the muddy bottom, the Comanches secured these items and rode back toward the south.

Except for small bands of plains Indians and occasional travelers or soldiers, this part of Texas was seldom visited. As a result, the two wagons caught in the shallow lake bed went unnoticed for decades. Over time, the wooden planks rotted away, spilling the shipment of gold onto the floor of the lake. The heavy weight and high density of the precious metal caused it to sink out of sight beneath the soft, saturated sands of the playa.

According to available records, Shafter and his command never ventured back to the lake which now bears his name. Military assignments kept him from returning to the region. One of them was to lead a company of cavalry on the island of Cuba during the Santiago Campaign in 1898. Shafter died in 1906. It is reasonable to assume the huge shipment of gold was never retrieved by the only person who was aware of its location.

�֎

During the summer of 1901, a few pieces of rotted wagon timber were found in the middle of a dry playa bed in West Texas by a man named William Russell. Russell, along with his wife and three children, were traveling from Denton, Texas, to Pecos when their wagon broke down northeast of Andrews near a dry lake bed. Russell set up camp, and while he and his wife made repairs to the wagon, his sons explored the crusty surface of the playa. During their evening meal, Russell noticed one of his sons playing with some items he had never before seen. When he examined them, he realized they were pieces of harness and wagon fittings. When Russell asked his son where he found them, the boy pointed toward the middle of the nearby playa and stated they were just lying on the surface.

The next morning before continuing with repairs on the wagon, Russell walked out into the playa. Near the middle, he discovered the rotted and rusted remains of at least two wagons, as well as some weathered bones of horses and mules. As Russell looked around the area, he was unaware that only a few inches beneath his feet lay a fortune in gold.

Russell completed repairs on his wagon and proceeded to Pecos where he eventually established a successful commercial orchard and truck garden. Approximately ten years after settling into the small West Texas town, Russell told a friend about finding pieces of wagons out on the dry lake bed near Andrews. The friend then related a story he once heard from a former black cavalryman about two wagonloads of gold that had sunk into the lake and which had to be abandoned because of an Indian attack.

Russell was excited about the possibility of returning to the playa and retrieving what he knew must be an amazing fortune. Several weeks later, Russell, along with his two sons, traveled by wagon to the playa that was now known throughout the region as Shafter Lake. On arriving, however, they found the lake filled with water to the depth of three feet, the result of recent heavy rains and runoff in the region. Russell remained encamped by the shore for several days while he attempted to formulate some strategy to retrieve the gold. Finally, he gave up and retuned to Pecos. Russell made several more trips to Shafter Lake, but each time found it filled with water.

In 1931, an unnamed ranch hand told a story in Andrews that, while he was out searching for some stray cattle two weeks earlier, he was crossing the dry lake bed north of town when he found several pieces of an old wagon scattered across the playa. Two ranchers who overheard the story were familiar with the tale of Pecos Bill's lost gold and traveled out to the playa the next morning. The day was particularly windy, and by the time they reached it, the lake bed was completely covered by sand blown in by the strong West Texas winds. They found nothing.

When Shafter Lake fills with water following heavy rains, the porous sand and silt of the bottom expands. As a result, heavy objects at the surface sink easily into the saturated, loosely consolidated mud. While some researchers agree that the Shafter gold has long since sunk into this soil, there is little agreement as to the depth it may have reached, with estimates ranging from a few inches to in excess of four feet.

After securing permission to explore the private property on which Shafter Lake is located, at least two expeditions have employed metal detectors in an attempt to locate the metal. While bits and pieces of harnesses and other metal fittings were found, the gold eluded the searchers, suggesting that it had sunk beyond the range of the electronic equipment.

With recent advances in metal detecting and related technology occurring every day, it may be just a matter of time before Shafter Lake yields Pecos Bill's long-lost treasure.

5

THE LOST DUTCHMAN MINE OF
THE SUPERSTITION MOUNTAINS

In the minds of many, the most famous lost mine in the United States is the one called the Lost Dutchman Mine located somewhere in the Superstition Mountains of Arizona. As a result of feature films as well as numerous books and articles, this lost mine has received a great deal of attention and has captured the imagination of the public. With the passage of so much time, it is often difficult to separate fact from legend, but the prevailing truth is that this mine, actually several mines, did exist. A further truth is that, according to research, these mines were played out and likely no longer yielded any ore. However, a great portion of the gold that was taken from these mines remains in the area buried in a number of secret locations, an amount that would be equal to many millions of dollars today. This ore has been found and lost, and continues to lure hopeful searchers to this day.

The mysterious setting of the Superstition Mountains seems an appropriate place for a tale of lost gold. Once a homeland for Apache Indians, this desert region manifests extremely rugged terrain, steep slopes, sharp ridges, extreme aridity, and populations of rattlesnakes, scorpions, and poisonous centipedes.

Long before this region came to the notice of the gold-seeking Spanish explorers during the early 1700s, the area's Indian tribes believed the region to be inhabited by several different gods, all of which protected the gold. The Indians believed that the Superstition Mountains were ruled by a deity they called the Thunder God. They claimed he had the power to hurl rocks from cliff tops onto any and all who dared enter the region in search of the precious ore. It was from this, as well as other Indian legends, that the so-called Curse of the Superstition Mountains derived its origins.

In addition to the Apaches, the Pima Indians offered their own legend. They believed that when the Aztec leader Montezuma gathered up his followers along with his huge fortune, he journeyed from deep in Mexico northward into the Superstition Mountains. Here, claim the Pimas, Montezuma buried uncountable millions of dollars' worth of gold, silver, and jewels. Montezuma selected the Superstitions because he believed that in the remote sanctuary it would be safe from raiders.

Montezuma had not expected the Spaniards. Under the command of Coronado, the Spanish explorers entered the region during the early 1500s. In 1539, one expedition led by Fray Marcos de Niza set forth from Mexico City in an attempt to locate a quantity of gold believed to exist somewhere in the vast region of the northern desert. Accompanying de Niza were miners, geologists, and engineers. For years afterward, prospecting and mining activity provided for the opening of hundreds of productive mines throughout much of the American Southwest. Gold and silver were discovered in several locations.

A number of successful shaft and placer mining operations were undertaken in the Superstition Mountains of Arizona. Gold was processed, formed into ingots, and accumulated. Every two or three months, pack trains carrying hundreds of ingots plied the hazardous trails from the mines to governmental and church headquarters in Mexico City.

As the Spanish mining activity in the Superstition Mountains increased, so did Apache resentment of the intruders. The Indians long considered the range their homeland as well as a holy ground, and the growing encroachment of the newcomers was testing the patience of the tribe. In their quest for providing food for the miners and attendant populations, the Spaniards were decimating herds of deer and bison to the degree that little remained for the Indians. As time went by, the Apaches grew frustrated and began to retaliate. At first, small hunting parties were ambushed along narrow trails. As the ranks of the Spaniards were thinned over time, the Indians began attacking the mining camps.

Daylong battles ensued with regularity, with the Spanish generally suffering the greatest losses.

In spite of the Indian threat, and with occasional reinforcements, the Spanish continued to work the mines until the mid-1700s. At that time, as a result of the gradual depletion of the large deposits of ore, along with the continued Indian raids, the Spanish began the gradual process of abandoning the area. Prior to leaving, the Spaniards, considering the possibility of returning to the area someday to resume mining operations, covered all of the entrances to the shafts in the hope that this would deter any who followed them into the range in pursuit of gold.

For years, the Superstition Mountains remained quiet and undisturbed. Few other than Apache Indians passed through the area, and they remained constantly on guard against the return of the intruding miners. Unknown to the Indians at the time, the Mexican Revolution of 1821 marked the end of the Spanish reign in the region, thus prohibiting them from returning to the mountains to extract more of the gold.

Many years later in Mexico, a man named Peralta learned of the rich gold mines in the Superstition Mountains that the Spanish had been forced to abandon. For decades, the Peralta family operated several successful gold mines in the Mexican state of Sonora as well as southern Arizona, which at the time was part of Mexico. They became intrigued with the possibility of extending their interests into the Superstition Mountains. After obtaining geological, geographical, and engineering information on the Superstition mines, Don Miguel Peralta II organized a party to travel to the isolated and still dangerous range with the hope of locating gold and reopening the existing shafts.

During the following months, Peralta employed geologists, engineers, and laborers as well as dozens of armed guards for protection against marauding Indians. By the time the Peralta expedition departed Mexico for the Superstition Mountains, it numbered over four hundred men.

On arriving in the range the Peralta Expedition, employing the Spanish maps, relocated several placer mines and reopened some of the more productive shafts. The laborers worked as long as eighteen hours each day, seven days per week.

As it turned out, mining gold in the Superstition range was as profitable for Peralta as it had been for the Spaniards, and an immense fortune in the ore had been mined and shipped from the range. During the 1840s Peralta, now in his sixties, learned of the impending Treaty of Hidalgo, an agreement that would grant that part of Mexico to the United States. The treaty was to take effect in 1848, so Peralta hurried to mine as much gold as he could before being forced from the area.

In addition to having to deal with the approaching deadlines of the treaty, Peralta also had to contend with the growing number of raids by the Indians. Miners, guards, and hunters often fell victim to Apache arrows. Over time, talk of the Curse of the Superstition Mountains occupied the conversations of the Mexicans.

As the time to depart the area approached, Peralta, like the Spanish before him, covered and camouflaged all of the mine shafts, believing it would serve as a deterrent to others who might come to the range in search of the gold. Peralta was hopeful he would be able to return and reopen the mines in the future.

After having tons of gold loaded onto mules, Peralta transported his wealth back to Mexico via a series of pack trains. Because time was limited, and because of the abundance of gold and the shortage of mules, Peralta was forced to bury millions of dollars' worth of ore at a number of secret locations not far from the shafts.

One such pack train consisting of twenty mules, each carrying heavy leather sacks filled with gold ore and led by a contingent of armed and mounted guards, wound its way through the canyons and out of the range on its way to Mexico City. As mules and guards passed single file along a narrow trail that paralleled Camp Creek, they were ambushed by Apaches.

Panicked, the guards bolted, only to be overtaken by the Indians and slaughtered. Moments later, the excited and milling mules were rounded up. The Apaches considered mule meat a delicacy and were anxious to herd the animals back to their campground. On the other hand, the Indians cared little for gold other than for ornaments such as armbands and necklaces. Within minutes, they cut the packs away and scattered the gold in the creek bed. To this day, hikers along Camp Creek still pick up gold nuggets from the sands and gravels of this ephemeral stream.

Shortly after the Treaty of Hidalgo was signed, gold was discovered in California and the great gold rush was on. These two events eventually brought together Peralta and a German immigrant named Jacob Walz (sometimes spelled Waltz and Waltzer). Walz would soon become the most prominent figure associated with the Superstition gold mines.

Walz arrived on the eastern seaboard of the United States with many years of mining experience. He was immediately employed at gold mines in North Carolina and Georgia. Walz was living in Mississippi when he learned of the fabulous gold discoveries in California. Along with thousands of others, Walz packed his bag and headed west in hope of striking it rich.

Little is known of Walz's activities prior to 1860. He was purported to be a recluse and for the most part shunned contact with other men. It is believed he worked several small but unproductive placer claims in northern California. Here he was known as the Dutchman, a nickname that stuck with him for the rest of his life.

According to legend, Walz was enjoying a beer in a tavern in some small mining town in California when he was distracted by a disturbance. At the opposite end of the bar, a drunk and angry gambler was beating on an elderly man. When the gambler plunged a knife into the stomach of the defenseless man, Walz stepped in and wrestled the weapon away. He picked up the bleeding victim and carried him to his hotel room where he treated the wound. Over the next few days, the old man recovered as Walz tended to him and brought him meals.

The old man introduced himself to Walz as Don Miguel Peralta II and the two became friends. When Peralta was fully recovered, he told Walz about his rich gold mines in the Superstition Mountains of Arizona. At first, Walz did not believe the old man, but Peralta eventually provided him with directions as well as a map showing the locations of several of the still productive mines that had been covered over along with a number of the buried caches.

A short time later as the War Between the States gained momentum, Walz, using the map and directions provided by Peralta, traveled to the Superstition Mountains to search for the gold mines. He had difficulty interpreting Peralta's map, but after several years of searching finally found gold. In the western end of the range near the normally dry Camp Creek, Walz found much of the ore earlier scattered by the Apaches following the ambush. In addition, he located a significant placer deposit.

Not far from Camp Creek, Walz encountered the ruins of several rock houses in which Peralta's miners and guards once lived. Not far from these, he located two shafts that had been covered over. From where he stood near these shafts, Walz could see the sharply pointed peak off to the south that a number of researchers have identified as Weavers Needle, a prominent landmark in the area. Other investigators, however, are convinced that Walz was looking at Pinnacle Peak. After exploring the region for several days, Walz found at least two of the large caches of ore and ingots that had been buried by Peralta.

Once Walz determined that he had indeed found Peralta's mining claim, he set about panning gold from some of the streams and reopening the mine shafts. As he panned and dug ore, he allegedly cached quantities of it alongside Peralta's stashes in other places. According to research, the only time Walz ever left the range was to travel to Phoenix to purchase supplies.

While in town, Walz always paid for his purchases with gold. According to many, they were the purest nuggets ever seen in the region. When townsfolk asked Walz about the source of his gold, he refused to talk about it, saying only that no one would ever find his mines. As in California, he was known locally as the Dutchman.

When more people became aware of Walz's mining successes, some began following him on his return trips to the Superstition Mountains. Walz expected such a thing to happen and he devised a number of ways to elude his trackers. It has been said that several men who set out on the trail of the Dutchman were never seen again. Many were convinced that Walz hid in ambush and killed them. Such tales added to the growing mystery about the Curse of the Superstition Mountains.

For twenty years Walz extracted gold from the mines and panned it from the streams. As he aged, his health began to fail and a variety of infirmities began taking a toll. During his last few years in the range, Walz dropped a few hints relative to the locations of some of his mines, but he shared precise directions with only one person, a woman he had befriended years earlier.

Julia Thomas owned a Phoenix ice cream parlor and was one of the few black women in the area. Most believe that the directions Walz provided Thomas were accurate because he would have no reason to deceive her. Paraphrased, the directions are as follows:

Follow the Salt River from Phoenix until arriving at a junction with a well-traveled trail. Take the trail to Sombrero Peak, and from this point continue to the eye of the Needle. From the eye, the mines lie almost due north. Continue to Blacktop Hill, thence to Blacktop Mesa. On the mesa can be seen an old stone corral left by the Spaniards. Cross the mesa and continue down the opposite side where a spring can be seen. Follow the trail northward until coming to another spring. Beyond this spring lies a canyon, and the mines are located at the head of it.

Walz also provided Thomas other information: that placer gold could be found at various locations in the dry stream bed that ran along the canyon floor; that the entrance to one important shaft was on the north-facing slope near the head of the canyon. Walz explained that one could stand as close as ten feet to the opening of the mine and still not see it. Inside, he said, was an eighteen-inch-thick vein of almost pure gold. Standing in front of the opening, one could look out across the small valley and see the ruins of an old rock house originally constructed by the Spaniards. At the top of the slope beyond the rock house was another shaft, this one vertical and also containing a thick seam of gold.

Other directions to Walz's gold exist, many of them cobbled together from the hints he left during his trips to town. Many of them contradict one another, and most are believed to be hoaxes.

Jacob Walz passed away in 1891 in the home of Thomas. With his death came the growing and often exaggerated tales of his gold. As a result, numerous expeditions entered the Superstition Mountains in search of what came to be called the Lost Dutchman Mine, the name by which it is best known today. Instead of a single mine, however, Walz's holdings included several shafts, a number of placer deposits, and numerous caches.

From that time until today, hundreds of expeditions have been launched into the Superstition Mountains in search of the Lost Dutchman Mine. Dozens of men have lost their lives. During the early years, some were victims of Indian attack. Others perished from thirst, snakebite, exposure, or falls from cliffs. Those who died were believed by many to be victims of the fabled curse.

Today there exist dozens of books and thousands of articles about the Lost Dutchman Mine and several movies have been made, all of which add to the legend. Despite all of the attention given to the tale, and despite the endless quests to find the gold, the sources of the ore have remained lost. Many contend Walz covered and camouflaged the mine shafts before he died. Others suggest they were covered by landslides generated by an earthquake in 1877. Still others will argue that the gold in the mines was simply depleted as a result of the mining activities by the Spaniards, Peralta, and Walz. And there are even some who claim the gold never existed at all.

That the Spaniards found gold in the Superstition Mountains cannot be denied; it is a matter of historical record. The same can be said for the huge mining operations conducted by Don Miguel Peralta II. That Walz found gold in the range is an established fact.

The truth is, the canyon containing the mine shafts and the placer deposits has been found several times over the years by prospectors and treasure hunters. While there is evidence that many of the mines have simply played out, the fact remains that the caches secreted by Peralta and Walz have not been located. It is these sources of gold ore, along with the opportunity to recover gold from Camp Creek, that continue to lure gold-seeking adventurers into the rugged vastness of the Superstition Mountains.

Men still arrive in the range today, each coming with the belief that they will be the lucky one to find gold. Most come away empty-handed. Some never return alive, for the ongoing threats of rattlesnake bite and thirst remain. It is not uncommon to read about another hiker who has lost his life in the Superstition range. Many say accidents are inevitable. Others claim the deaths are a result of poor preparation. And there are some who maintain that all were victims of the curse.

6

THE HUACHUCA
CANYON TREASURE

The state of Arizona is replete with legends of lost mines and buried treasures. Though none are as famous as that of the Lost Dutchman Mine, there exist others equally, if not more, fascinating—and promising. One of those that promises wealth beyond imagination to whomever finds it is known as the Huachuca Canyon Treasure, which consists of untold millions of dollars' worth of gold ingots. Finding this incredible hoard is not the main obstacle, for the location is known. Recovering it, however, is fraught with challenge and obstacles.

❖

Robert Jones was an enlisted man in the U.S. Army and was assigned to a communications division at Fort Huachuca in southeastern Arizona during the months leading up to World War II. During his stay there, the summer daytime temperatures rose to well over 100 degrees. On one of his days off, Jones decided to seek some relief from the heat by hiking and exploring the shady oak and pine canyons of the nearby Huachuca Mountains. Accompanied by a friend, he drove into Huachuca Canyon along a very old and seldom used dirt road.

Arriving at a point where the road had washed out, Jones parked his car and the two men continued up the canyon on foot along a shadowed trail. Now and again they spotted deer in the forest, squirrels and blue jays in the trees, and chipmunks among the rocks. Wary of rattlesnakes known to inhabit the area, they proceeded with caution.

As the two men made their way up the canyon, Jones noted changes in the color of the rock near the base of the rock wall. A large pile of loose rubble appeared to be talus from a former mining operation. Jones searched the area near the wastes but could not see evidence of a mine shaft. Curious, he climbed up the talus slope for a closer look. As Jones was walking along a short stretch of the canyon atop the talus, the ground suddenly gave way beneath him and he dropped thirty-two feet into an almost vertical shaft.

Stunned and slightly injured, Jones called out to his companion. By the time his friend arrived, Jones realized he had fallen into an old mine shaft, one that had been covered over sometime in the distant past. From where he sat at the bottom of the drop, Jones could see that the shaft leveled off and continued laterally into the bedrock of the mountain.

Responding to Jones's request, the friend retrieved a small flashlight from the vehicle and dropped it down to him. Pointing the narrow beam, Jones followed it into the passageway for twenty yards, eventually arriving at a low-ceilinged, rectangular chamber that had been excavated out of the rock and reinforced with hand-laid stones, mortar, and timbers. Jones, who was five feet seven inches tall, could barely stand upright in the chamber.

Employing the dim illumination of the flashlight, Jones explored the chamber. As he approached one of the walls, he saw that stacked along its length were what he determined were gold and silver ingots. They were twenty inches long and he estimated there were two hundred of each. He picked up one of the gold bars and hefted it. He estimated that it weighed fifty pounds.

Near the center of chamber, Jones encountered two large wooden tubs. Each one, he explained later, was "as big as three washtubs." One of the tubs was filled to the top with gold nuggets, the other half full with gold dust. A short distance from the tubs he found a large glass jar. Examining it in the glow of the flashlight, Jones saw that it contained what he thought was a message. With great care, he withdrew what he later described was a rolled up sheepskin on which was Spanish writing and a crude map. Unable to understand any of it, Jones placed it back into the jar and returned it to where he found it.

Jones was in the chamber for almost an hour when the flashlight began to fail. With difficulty, and with the help of his friend, he managed to climb out of the shaft. Excited, Jones told his companion what he had found inside the old mine shaft. He described what he estimated to be an incredible fortune in gold and silver ingots. As they hiked back to the location where the car was parked, the two friends made plans to return to the site and carry away as much of the gold and silver as they could manage.

Later that same afternoon when they returned to the military base, Jones and his friend sought out the company commander. After arranging a meeting, Jones explained what he found in Huachuca Canyon. The captain refused to believe any of what the sergeant told him and after a few minutes dismissed him. The two enlisted men sought help from other officers, but were unable to convince any of them of the existence of the treasure.

The following day, Jones related his adventure and discovery to First Sergeant Matt Venable. Years later when Venable was interviewed about his connection to the Huachuca Canyon treasure, he recalled that both Jones and his friend were exceptional soldiers and never known to exaggerate. After listening to Jones's tale, Venable made a recommendation to military authorities that they consider investigating the claim. No action was taken.

Discouraged, Jones and his friend decided to bide their time and wait for the appropriate opportunity to return to the canyon and retrieve the gold and silver. The next weekend, they made their way back to the site and determined that it lay within the boundaries of the military reservation. While there, they covered the opening with logs and branches to keep others from finding it. On a nearby tree, Jones made two slashes. Using a rock hammer, he scraped his initials on a granite boulder it was necessary to pass in order to get to the opening of the concealed mine.

Jones and his friend intended to undertake a retrieval operation as soon as possible. They identified digging and mining equipment necessary to accomplish their goal. They lay awake nights talking about what they would do with the treasure once they recovered it from the old mine. When they finally fell asleep, their dreams were of wealth.

The plans had to be postponed. A few months later, war was declared and Jones and his friend were transferred out of southeastern Arizona. Jones was shipped to the Pacific and his friend sent to the African-European theater. Within a few days of arriving at his new assignment, Jones's friend was killed. A short time later, Jones was severely wounded in a firefight on Wake Island. He spent several months recovering.

The need for medical treatment, therapy, and the financial difficulties it entailed kept Jones from returning to Huachuca Canyon. Eventually, he was discharged from the army and was given a small pension. He and his wife moved to Dallas, Texas, where she was employed as a nurse at the Dallas Medical Center.

The rehabilitation required by his wounds occupied Jones for the next eleven years. Despite everything, he remained crippled. Unable to exercise, Jones gained weight and had extreme difficulty getting around. During this time he returned to Huachuca Canyon several times, but he was unable to perform the work necessary to retrieve the treasure. In time, he formally appealed to the U.S. Army for assistance, but in every case he was informed he would not be allowed to dig for treasure on a military reservation.

In 1959 Jones sought an audience with Major General F. W. Moorman, who was the post commander of Fort Huachuca at the time. Unlike the officers he spoke with before, Moorman believed Jones's story. He examined Jones's military record and discovered he had been a competent and reliable soldier. Moorman arranged to have two military psychiatrists interview and evaluate Jones. Both reported that the subject was likely telling the truth about what he claimed he discovered in the old mine shaft. With this information, along with other documents supporting Jones's credibility, Moorman approved his application to attempt a recovery of the treasure believed to lie within the old mine shaft in Huachuca Canyon. A period of two weeks was granted for the project.

Jones formed a small company to administer and oversee the recovery attempt. Each member was to share in the wealth that was retrieved. On the morning of the first day of the allotted period, the group entered Huachuca Canyon. The participants followed Jones, who limped his way along the route using a cane, and eventually came to the boulder where he had caved his initials eighteen years earlier. Nearby were found the two slashes he made on the tree. A few minutes later, Jones was standing atop the logs and branches and other forest debris he and his friend had laid across the opening of the old mine. The material was pulled away, and moments later two of the team members descended into the shaft.

As they climbed down into the shaft, the men noted that it was clearly manmade and at least two hundred years old, maybe more. Halfway down they encountered a problem. Since Jones climbed out of the vertical shaft nearly two decades earlier, a portion of it had collapsed, filling the bottom with tons of rock. The treasure recovery team was now faced with the huge task of removing large and heavy rock in order to gain access to the treasure chamber. The equipment they carried with them was not up to this task. After returning to Fort Huachuca, Jones petitioned the military for permission to bring some heavy excavation equipment into the area in order to remove the rock fill. The army agreed to his plan but only at his own expense.

On hearing of Jones's plight, Moorman took pity on him and authorized the use of a military bulldozer that was brought to the site. With the bulldozer, much of the talus was cleared away and the opening of the shaft enlarged. Approximately half of the rock debris that had accumulated in the bottom of the shaft was removed. At that point, however, the diggers encountered another problem, a serious one. The remainder of the vertical shaft was not only filled with boulders but also with water, making further excavation difficult to impossible.

The operation was halted. Jones preoccupied himself with formulating alternative plans, but by the time he had come up with a new strategy for recovering the treasure, his allotted time had expired and he was ordered to vacate the canyon.

During the month of September 1959, Jones and his team returned to Fort Huachuca to attempt to negotiate another attempt at recovering the treasure. His request was granted, and Jones ordered a drilling rig to be transported to the site. With the rig, he succeeded in boring a hole into the main chamber where the gold and silver were stored. Jones reasoned that if water was located here then it could be pumped out through the hole while the debris filling the shaft was removed. As water pumps were being hooked up to generators, two bulldozers worked to enlarge the shaft and remove the boulders blocking the team's access. It would just be a matter of time, Jones was convinced, before they would reach the gold and silver ingots.

When another dozen feet of rock debris had been cleared from the entrance, another problem arose—water began seeping in at a faster rate. More pumps were brought to the site and work continued around the clock for the next three days and nights.

To the dismay of the engineer and geologist on the team, the seeping water was causing minor cave-ins in the old and highly weathered granite. The situation had become so dangerous that the recovery attempt was abandoned. Jones retreated to consider other strategies.

During the lull in the digging, Jones brought in another professional geologist to consult on the project. Following an inspection of the site, he agreed that they were digging into a manmade shaft, most likely one that had been excavated by early Spanish miners in this area. The geologist also declared the site unsafe and recommended the area be abandoned and sealed off.

Jones was not to be deterred, and after all of the equipment and personnel were removed from the area, he began to consider other options. By now, however, the activity in Huachuca Canyon and the revelation of the possibility of a huge treasure being found there attracted the attention of newspaper and television reporters from around the country. They arrived in large numbers to cover the progress of the recovery operation. As their numbers swelled in the canyon, military officials grew concerned about safety and security and threatened to terminate any and all excavation activity.

As reporters swarmed into the region, a representative from the U.S. Treasury Department arrived at the site and announced that he was empowered to assume possession of any and all treasure that might be recovered. Following an inventory of the hoard, he said 60 percent of whatever was found would go directly to the government. Jones would be eligible to receive the remaining 40 percent but it would be taxed.

Two weeks later, a large crane with a clam shovel was transported to the site. With the crane, another five feet of debris was removed. At this point, the workers encountered an exceptionally large boulder that had become wedged tight at the bottom of the shaft near the point where it went from vertical to horizontal. In order to reduce the resistance, a hole was bored into the rock and stuffed with explosive material. The subsequent blast created more problems than it solved—tons of adjacent rock were dislodged and collapsed into the shaft, completely refilling it. According to the consulting geologist, it was likely that the chamber containing the gold and silver ingots had also collapsed.

For another five days, men and machines labored to remove the additional rock. As they worked, they discovered that all traces of the original shaft had been obliterated. At this point, Jones was forced to abandon the project. Jones informed military authorities that he would attempt to acquire additional backing for another attempt at retrieving the treasure. The army decision makers, however, informed him that under no circumstances would he be allowed to dig in Huachuca Canyon again.

In spite of the decree from the military, Jones continued to solicit investors and apply for permission to excavate for the treasure he knew lay under hundreds of tons of rock and rubble. A few months later he found an ally in the Post Inspector General, Colonel Ethridge Bacon. Bacon was convinced that the treasure Jones spoke of existed. Though he made several tries, Bacon was never able to convince his superiors that Jones should be granted permission for another attempt. Two years later, Robert Jones died in his sleep in Dallas.

The search for the Huachuca Canyon treasure did not end with the death of Robert Jones. In 1975, the U.S. Army granted permission to Quest Exploration, a California-based treasure hunting company, to try to reach the cache of gold and silver. Quest employed state-of-the-art computerized sensing equipment to determine the location of the chamber described by Jones. During their search, however, Quest officials were informed by the army that any treasure recovered would be placed in escrow until all claims for it were settled in a court of law.

After a week of working at the site, the Quest team abandoned the project; they were not satisfied with the recovery terms. Before leaving the area, they stated that whatever openings and passageways may have existed had most certainly caved in as a result of previous excavation and demolition work.

After the Quest Exploration team left the site, the military closed off Huachuca Canyon and forbade access to treasure hunters. During a final sweep of the canyon, military policemen encountered a small mine shaft nearby in which were found several very old digging tools, a number of Spanish coins, and some glassware. When the find was reported, the officer in charge confiscated the items and instructed the MPs to keep the discovery secret.

The official position of the U.S. Army is that the treasure cache described by Robert Jones does not exist. Unofficially, however, the military continued to attempt to recover the gold and silver as late as 1979. During the autumn of that year, a squirrel hunter who frequented the canyon observed army bulldozers and other heavy equipment working around the site of the old shaft that Robert Jones had fallen into thirty-eight years earlier.

That Robert Jones stumbled into an old mine that contained a fortune in gold and silver ingots in Huachuca Canyon cannot be doubted; the evidence, along with his lifetime commitment to recovering the treasure, is overwhelming. Without a doubt, the mine was operated by the Spanish who were known to frequent this area. Evidence also shows that members of the U.S. military were convinced of Jones's assertions regarding the treasure cache, even to the point of organizing their own attempt at recovering it. It is known that they invested significant time, energy, and resources into the attempt. Subsequent visitors to the site in Huachuca Canyon have observed that, despite their efforts, the army has never been able to penetrate the mass of rock in order to achieve access to the underground chamber. For all indications, it is apparent that the fabulous Huachuca Canyon treasure has never been recovered and still lies there today in the ruined chamber under tons of rock and rubble.

7

SEVENTEEN TONS OF GOLD AT LOST MESA

One of the largest caches of gold in the history of the United States is located on a mesa in a remote portion of the desert in San Juan County in the Four Corners region of northwestern New Mexico. During the mid-1930s, approximately seventeen tons of gold were flown in several trips to this region from deep in Mexico. The gold was delivered to and buried at the top of an isolated flat-topped mountain where it was to be held until certain economic circumstances materialized. When such circumstances were not forthcoming, the parties involved in the caching of this incredible fortune were forced to abandon the site, never to return. According to all available information, the gold is still there. The principal difficulty related to locating and recovering it is in determining which mesa is the correct one. If found, the value of the gold would equal that of the treasury of a midsize nation.

During the summer of 1933, William C. Elliot received an odd telegram at the office of the small crop-dusting service he owned and operated in Midvale, Utah, a few miles south of Salt Lake City. The telegram was from a man named Don Leon Trabuco and it was an invitation for Elliot to fly to a small landing strip near Kirtland, New Mexico, for a meeting. Elliot, who was known as Wild Bill among his pilot friends, had never heard of Don Trabuco, but the message informed him he was to be paid twenty-five hundred dollars for his troubles. He was also instructed to tell no one of the arrangement. The message carried neither information regarding the subject of the meeting nor an explanation as to why Elliot was selected to attend.

Elliot was more than qualified as a pilot. A native of Salt Lake City, he had been employed as a stunt flyer for a circus, at one time owned a charter service, and was currently working as a crop duster helping Utah farmers fight the plague of crickets that was devastating much of the state's agricultural productivity. Having never made much money at his flying enterprises, Elliot was lured by the large fee and agreed to make the seven-hundred-mile round trip.

Two days later Elliot landed at the tiny Kirtland airstrip. As he was climbing out of his plane, he noticed a tall man in a dark suit walking toward him. The man was a Mexican. Without speaking, he handed Elliot a typed note. It was from Don Trabuco and carried instructions to meet him at the Kirtland Hotel. The Mexican motioned the pilot toward a waiting automobile.

Don Leon Trabuco had a home near the city of Puebla, Mexico. There, Trabuco owned vast parcels of land and ranches. He was also a banker and operated several successful businesses in Puebla. When he met Elliot at the hotel, Trabuco, along with his aides, were expensively dressed. All were very polite, and all spoke English as though they had been educated in the United States. It was rumored that Trabuco was descended from the original Spanish conquistadores who conquered Mexico centuries earlier. It was also told that he was the head of a large, prominent, and extremely powerful family that controlled the politics and economics throughout much of the region where he lived.

As Trabuco spoke, one of his assistants handed Elliot a flight map of an area near Puebla where one of Trabuco's large ranches was located. Here, Trabuco told the pilot, he was to land his plane and pick up a cargo of gold ingots. After leaving the ranch, Elliot was to fly an evasive pattern back to New Mexico and land at a remote airstrip near a small isolated mesa located a few miles northwest of the town of Shiprock. The assistant pointed out fuel stops along the return route.

Trabuco told Elliot that if he were pleased with his compensation this would be the first of several trips, and that ultimately a total of seventeen tons of gold was to be delivered to the designated site over a period of several weeks. For his efforts, Trabuco told Elliot he would be paid forty thousand dollars in cash. He also informed him that this, and any future business conducted between the two men, was to be kept secret.

Elliot thought about the proposition. Mentally, he calculated how many planes he would be able to purchase and how he could improve and expand his crop-dusting business. Following a few minutes of deliberation, Elliot agreed to the arrangement. Smiling, Trabuco told Elliot to fly his plane to the Puebla ranch the next day. He then handed the pilot twenty-five hundred dollars in cash.

Late afternoon of the following day, Elliot landed his plane and pulled to a stop at the end of a short landing strip near the Trabuco ranch house in Mexico. Within seconds, a number of uniformed guards carrying machine guns met him and instructed him to stand to one side while they monitored the loading of a number of heavy gold ingots into the plane by three laborers. This done, Elliot was shown his quarters and fed dinner.

The next morning after breakfast, Elliot took off and flew the prescribed route back to New Mexico. During the 1930s, eluding the border patrol and other law enforcement authorities was a simple task. This done, he eventually landed his plane at a tiny, rough and rocky makeshift landing strip adjacent to the specified mesa.

By the time Elliot cut his engines, a brand-new pickup truck was driven to the side of the plane. From the cab stepped Don Trabuco himself and two of his assistants. This time, Trabuco was dressed in work clothes: khakis, a safari jacket, and high-topped boots. Elliot noted that there were several shovels and other excavation tools in the bed of the truck.

Elliot was ordered to stand several yards away from the planes as the two assistants unloaded the gold and placed it in the back of the truck. The gold, explained Trabuco, was to be driven to a secret location atop the mesa, wrapped and sealed with wax, and buried. Trabuco informed Elliot he would be contacted within the next few days regarding the next pickup and delivery of gold. The two men shook hands. As Elliot took off and made the turn to head back to Midvale, he observed the vehicle carrying the gold ingots laboring up a narrow and switch-backing rock and dirt road that led up the steep incline toward the top of the mesa.

During the next several weeks, Elliot made a total of sixteen trips to Puebla and back. He estimated he had transported a total of 350 gold ingots, each of which he guessed weighed one hundred pounds.

Elliot grew curious about where the gold was being buried atop the mesa. After his plane was unloaded following one of his deliveries, he took off and circled the mesa twice as he gained altitude, eventually orienting his Cessna in a northwesterly direction toward Midvale and home. As the plane approached the mesa from the southeast, Elliot cut the engines and glided over the flat-surfaced landform in search of Trabuco's pickup truck. Gazing out the window, he finally spotted it near the western edge of the mesa. Even from this high altitude, he could see three men excavating what appeared to be a shallow trench.

When Elliot made his final delivery, he was invited to another meeting with Trabuco at the Kirtland Hotel. There, he was paid the forty thousand dollars in cash that was promised. He was also informed by Trabuco that in the event that the gold was eventually sold at a specified profit in the future he would be given a significant bonus.

For the next several years, Elliot kept up with the rising and falling prices of gold and observed that the stated expectations of Don Trabuco were never met. Elliot was disappointed, for he looked forward to the bonus he thought he would receive.

One evening, Elliot was reading the newspaper when he spotted an article that described how Don Leon Trabuco and several other prominent Mexican businessmen had been charged with corruption and conspiracy to murder. They were tried, found guilty, and sent to prison. For the next several months, Elliot attempted to keep himself informed of the situation in Mexico and occasionally received news that was provided by contacts he had in the area. One evening on returning home from a crop-dusting job, he received the news that Don Trabuco had died in prison.

Elliot was convinced that the seventeen tons of gold he delivered to the landing strip at Kirtland was still buried atop the remote mesa. He was determined to travel to the area and retrieve it for himself at the first available opportunity.

Time passed, and opportunities were not forthcoming. Elliot's newly expanded crop-dusting business, along with a charter flying service he started, was making significant profits and kept him busy. As a result, he found it difficult to leave long enough to attempt to retrieve the gold.

Years passed, and World War II broke out. The patriotic Elliot enlisted in the U.S. Army Air Corps. With his flying experience, he was sent immediately to the war theater in England. In December 1944, Elliot was reported missing in action. Two months later it was discovered that his plane had been shot down. He and his copilot were killed.

As far as can be determined, by 1950 all of the principals involved in caching the seventeen tons of gold atop the isolated mesa in northwestern New Mexico were either dead or far away in Mexico. According to some people who Elliot took into his confidence and told about the massive treasure, it likely still lies atop the mesa buried in the shallow trench.

Because so few people were aware of the existence of this incredible treasure cache, only a handful of adventurous individuals have undertaken a search for it. All were unsuccessful. The mesas found in northwestern New Mexico are rarely, if ever, visited and explored.

Elliot left no notes or maps related to the treasure, apparently trusting everything to memory. Most of the information about this multimillion-dollar cache came from sparse information that Elliot shared with a small number of friends.

What is known is that, while the mesa that houses this fabulous treasure is not the largest in the area, it still covers hundreds of acres. Other than that, the only other concrete information available is related to the fact that the treasure is still buried on the western end.

8

THE LOST TREASURE
OF CANCINO ARROYO

Cancino Arroyo is a winding, often deep gully located in Rio Arriba County in north-central New Mexico between the tiny town of Tres Piedras and the Rio Grande. There exists a compelling tale of dozens of gold ingots believed to be worth millions of dollars buried under a few feet of sand and gravel at the bottom of this arroyo. All who possessed intimate details of this lost treasure are long dead, though some of their offspring claim to have an idea of the general region where the treasure might be found. Well over a century of erosion and deposition, along with the soft, porous bottom of the arroyo, has hampered recovery operations that have been undertaken during the past decades.

Tres Piedras is a small village located about twenty-five miles from the Rio Grande. In this region, a number of deep, water-eroded arroyos wind their way from the higher elevation to the historic river. Water flows in these arroyos ephemerally, the result of occasional rains that visit the area. Most of the time, however, they are dry.

This tale has it origins in Cimarron, New Mexico, on August 9, 1880. Cimarron is located sixty miles east of Tres Piedras. A man named Porter Stockton, along with a companion named West, became embroiled in a dispute that ended in a gunfight. Stockton, a local ne'er-do-well with a reputation for robbery and murder, killed two men. Knowing he was in serious trouble, Stockton, accompanied by West, mounted his horse and fled westward to a hideout in Gallegos Canyon not far from Tres Piedras.

The two outlaws eventually crossed the Rio Grande and, after reaching the opposite bank, noted that storm clouds were forming in the northwest. After they had traveled another two miles a light rain began falling. For the rest of the day, the rain grew in intensity, making travel difficult. By nightfall, a raging storm struck the area and the dense rainfall reduced visibility to only a few feet. Much of the trail the two men were following was washed out and they soon found themselves lost. Seeking shelter, Stockton and West turned into a deep arroyo and followed its winding course, hoping it would come out on higher ground.

Unknown to Stockton and West, three riders were less than an hour behind them on the same trail. Like the two outlaws, these three men were lost and in search of shelter from the storm. Trailing behind the three men were two heavily laden mules on lead ropes, each one carrying a fortune in gold ingots. Weeks earlier, these same men had followed directions they had derived from an old and faded parchment map and located a large cache of Spanish gold hidden in an abandoned mine shaft far to the southwest in Arizona. After loading as many ingots as their leather panniers could hold, the trio set out on the long journey to their homes in Colorado, where they intended to sell the treasure and make plans to return to the cache and retrieve the remainder. They were less than one hundred miles from their destination when they were caught in the heavy storm.

Since none of them had visited that part of New Mexico before, the three newcomers became confused and disoriented when the trail they were following was washed away. Spotting the now vague tracks of Stockton and West, who had passed that way a short time earlier, and believing the riders must be familiar with the terrain, the trio turned into the arroyo and followed them.

As Stockton and West traveled up the arroyo, they noted that it grew deeper and narrower, the vertical walls stretching sixty feet high in some places. The normally dry stream bed accommodated a fast-moving current, and the roiling silt and sand bottom was nearly one foot deep and making travel difficult. Noting that the current was getting stronger and the water rising, Stockton suggested they turn around and return to the opening of the arroyo and seek a safer route. As the two outlaws retraced their path, occasional flashes of lighting illuminated the walls of the arroyo.

On rounding a bend in the channel, Stockton and West came face-to-face with the three riders who were making their way up the gully. Stockton assumed the men were part of a posse sent to capture or kill him and West. He yanked his revolver from its holster and fired, charging into the riders as he did so. West followed him.

The surprise encounter rendered the three riders stunned and helpless. Before they could regain their composure, all were lying dead, their bodies partially covered by the rising waters of the arroyo. Stockton and West also shot and killed the three horses and two mules, then fled as fast as they could toward the mouth of the arroyo and on to Gallegos Canyon.

Stockton and West, mistaking the three strangers for lawmen, were unaware that they had just ridden away from a fortune in gold.

As the two outlaws disappeared into the storm, the heavy rain continued to fall and dense sheets of runoff from the nearby slopes flowed into the numerous channels that fed the Rio Grande several miles away. Within an hour after the killing of the three men, Cancino Arroyo was inundated with a raging flash flood, with the surging water rising several feet up the vertical walls. These waters, carrying a heavy load of sediment, washed over the dead men, horses, and gold.

✥

The morning following the intense storm, the high desert around Tres Piedras was bathed in sunshine and cleansed air. Two Mexican sheepherders—an old man and a young boy—awoke from their storm-ravaged sleep. The limb- and grass-thatched lean-to in which they lived afforded scant protection from the downpour of the previous night. As the old man hung blankets out to dry and looked over at the herd of sheep entrusted to his care, he remarked to the boy that he thought he had heard gunfire during the night.

Two hours later, after making certain that none of the sheep were missing, the old man walked over to the rim of Cancino Arroyo and looked into the deep, shaded channel. A stream of water several inches deep still flowed along the bottom, and as the old man's eyes grew accustomed to the shadows below, he spotted what he thought were the bodies of three men and several horses partially submerged in the sand.

He called the boy over, and the two scrambled down a steep but negotiable bank of the arroyo and walked up to the grisly scene. Cutting open one of the leather packs that had not been completely buried, the sheepherder withdrew an eighteen-inch-long object that he believed to be a piece of iron. Curious, he sliced open the remaining packs only to find more of the same. Having no need for such metal, the herder tossed them to the ground. On an impulse, he stuck one of them in his sash, determined to keep it until such time as he might find a use for it. Finding nothing of value, the herder and the boy climbed back to the rim of the arroyo and returned to the job of caring for the sheep. As the old man passed the lean-to, he withdrew the piece of metal and tossed it inside amid his few belongings.

Later that afternoon, the rains returned. They were lighter than the previous day but lasted well into the night. That evening as the man and boy attempted to keep the cook fire going under the primitive lean-to, Cancino Arroyo was the scene of another flash flood. This time, with waters nearly ten feet deep, the stream raced and crashed along the bottom from wall to wall, sweeping away or covering everything in its path.

Around midmorning of the following day, Dolores Cancino, a rancher and owner of the sheep in the care of the old man and boy, arrived with supplies for the two herders. As he unloaded food and other items, the old man told the rancher what he had found at the bottom of the arroyo. When he had completed his report, he handed Cancino the piece of metal he retrieved. Cancino hefted the ingot, and scraped away at the surface with his thumbnail. A look of surprise washed over him as he realized the object he was holding was composed of almost pure gold.

After assigning the boy to watch over the sheep, Cancino and the old sheepherder returned to the bottom of the arroyo. Wading through the two-feet-deep water, they dug into the mud in an attempt to relocate the bodies of men and animals and the packs of gold. They found nothing. After returning to the top, Cancino decided to spend the night at the camp and make another attempt at finding the gold the next morning when he was certain the flow of water through the arroyo had ceased altogether.

Just after sunrise, Cancino and the old man were back in the arroyo, probing and digging in the sands but finding nothing. Cancino finally decided that the high-velocity waters of the flash flood of the previous night had carried away the corpses of men and animals as well as the packs of gold. Cancino rode a horse along the rim of the arroyo searching the stream bed for some sign. After traveling thirty yards he spotted one of the dead horses partially buried in the sand. Moments later he made his way to the bottom and found two more horses and a mule. The bodies of the three men were nowhere to be seen. None of the gold ingots were found.

One week later, Cancino drove his wagon to Santa Fe and turned the ingot over to a friend who agreed to have it assayed. When the report came in, it stated that the bar was composed of a high grade of gold and cast in a manner associated with early Spanish miners. The assayer said the ingot was worth just over two thousand dollars.

Over the next several months, Dolores Cancino explored up and down the bottom of the arroyo that bore his name but found nothing. When rains came and runoff flooded the bottom of the arroyo, Cancino would hurry to the area in hopes that the surging waters would wash away quantities of sand and silt and expose more of the gold ingots, but he had no luck.

In 1881, Cancino met Steve Upholt, a man with considerable mining experience. He told Upholt about the gold ingots he believed were lying under sand at the bottom of the arroyo and asked for his help in retrieving them. Upholt surprised Cancino by telling him that the gold was likely in the exact same place where it was originally dumped and that it had undoubtedly sunk several inches into the soft and yielding bottom of the arroyo. Upholt explained that when certain sands become saturated with water, they become unstable and turn into quicksand. Anything heavy, such as a gold ingot, would almost immediately sink to some depth below the surface.

Before the afternoon was over, Cancino and Upholt formed a partnership dedicated to a search for the gold. Two months later, Upholt arrived at the sheep camp near the rim of Cancino Arroyo and spent several days walking up and down the stream bed. Since the time the three unknown riders were killed and the gold dumped, a number of flash floods tearing through the narrow channel had created changes in the bottom and caused portions of the walls to collapse, all causing Upholt to believe the gold would be covered with more sand than he originally thought. This added to the difficulty of recovery, he explained. Furthermore, the configuration of the arroyo's channel had been modified to the degree that the old sheepherder could not be certain of the exact location of his original discovery of the bodies and the gold.

Time passed, and one afternoon while walking along the canyon bottom, Upholt chanced upon a partial human skeleton. After scraping away the covering of sand, he found some rotted clothes and boots still clinging to the frame. Encircling the pelvis was a cracked leather cartridge belt with a holster in which a revolver still resided. Upholt was convinced that this skeleton was what remained of one of the three men found in the arroyo two years earlier. If so, it had washed a considerable distance downstream. The next afternoon, Upholt hiked farther up the arroyo and found a second skeleton. After examining it closely, he discerned that it had a bullet hole in the skull. One week later and several more yards upstream, Upholt found the skeleton of the third man.

Upholt explained to Cancino that the bodies, being lighter than the gold, had been carried some distance downstream by the floodwaters. Because they were heavier, the horses and mules, he reasoned, would not have been carried as far as the men. He claimed that if he continued to search farther upstream he would likely find the skeletons of the animals. If this was borne out, he further reasoned, this would place them closer to where the gold was dropped.

Another week passed, and Upholt found a skeleton of one of the mules. Nearby, he also found a rotted packsaddle and a portion of a leather pannier. Studying his location, Upholt realized that if he traveled a short distance upstream he would be near the rim close to the sheep camp.

A few more days passed, and Upholt finally decided on a location where he thought he would have the best chance for finding the gold. He excavated three holes within a wide perimeter he outlined. The work was tedious and exhausting, but the miner was convinced that planning, patience, and persistence would lead him to the gold. When he had excavated each hole to the depth of six feet, he employed a probe to try to determine the depth of bedrock. He found it nine feet below. The bars of gold, he concluded, could possibly have sunk that far. Upholt was encouraged.

Two days later as Upholt widened and deepened the holes, he encountered his first gold ingot. It was seven feet below the surface of the channel. Convinced this was the correct location, he renewed his efforts and found two more ingots over the next two days.

When Dolores Cancino arrived at the site one week later, Upholt showed him a total of twelve gold ingots he had retrieved. The following morning, the two men traveled to Santa Fe, sold the gold, and divided the money. While in town, Upholt told Cancino it was necessary for him to go to Colorado to check on some ongoing mining interests he had there and that he would return as soon as possible. When he got back to the site at the arroyo, he suggested they hire some laborers to continue with the excavation. After the two men shook hands, Upholt drove away. He was never seen again, and his disappearance remains a mystery to this day.

Weeks passed, and when it became apparent to Cancino that Upholt would not be returning, he decided to resume the excavation himself. On arriving back at the arroyo, however, Cancino was discouraged to discover that subsequent flash floods had refilled Upholt's excavations and further modified the channel. Not long afterward, Cancino sold his ranch and his sheep herd and moved to Santa Fe, where he purchased and operated a grocery store. He remained there until he passed away thirteen years later. He never returned to Cancino Arroyo.

Cancino Arroyo, as it is still known today, remains remote to most travelers. It is, however, occasionally visited by hopeful treasure hunters who believe they might have a chance at recovering what remains of the lost gold ingots which are certain to lie several feet below the surface of the channel. The gold, estimated to be worth several million dollars, remains elusive.

9

THE LOST GRIERSON FORTUNE

During his lifetime as a successful farmer and businessman, John Grierson amassed an impressive fortune. Grierson, described as eccentric, inherited substantial wealth and then proceeded to make an additional fortune from cotton and livestock on his farm in Tazewell County, Virginia. Grierson owned thirty slaves, and around the time the War Between the States broke out he was thought to be one of the wealthiest men in Virginia. He was regarded as a millionaire, a staggering amount of money at the time.

As the war gained momentum, Grierson grew concerned that his farm, his home, and his fortune would attract raiding soldiers and renegades. He was also worried that the bank in town where most of his money was deposited would be a target for outlaws and Union troops. Grierson withdrew all of his money, converted it into gold coins, placed them into leather sacks, and with the help of a slave, buried them on his property behind his barn. There, this impressive treasure would have likely lain unknown to any and all were it not for the discovery of the diary of an old cowhand in West Texas.

✦

One autumn morning in 1887 on a remote ranch near Pecos, Texas, a young cowboy who had just been assigned to repair some fence at the east end of the ranch walked into the bunkhouse to wake his companion, an elderly man named John Crismo. When Crismo didn't respond, the boy walked over to his bunk and shook him. In a moment, he realized the old man was dead.

The ranch foreman was summoned. There was little to do but arrange for a burial. That afternoon, the owner of the ranch went through Crismo's belongings in search of the name of a relative who needed to be informed of the old man's death. He found nothing of interest until he came upon a diary. The rancher read it, and learned the fascinating details of Crismo's life along with a description of a buried treasure in faraway Virginia, a fortune worth millions of dollars lying buried beneath only a few inches of soil.

In 1846, when the United States declared war on Mexico, John Crismo enlisted in the army in his home state of New York. Before leaving with his company, Crismo became engaged to a young girl, and the two agreed to marry on his return. While Crismo was in Mexico, however, the young lady fell ill and died only days before he was to be mustered out of the military.

Dejected, Crismo made the long journey back to New York, visited the grave of his betrothed, and rode away, never to return. For years Crismo wandered about in the wilderness of Pennsylvania and Ohio, always keeping to himself and living deep in the woods, craving neither the sight nor company of other men.

When the War Between the States erupted, Crismo, harboring a desire to return to combat, rode into a Pennsylvania town and enlisted in the Union Army. He was assigned to a cavalry regiment and ordered to Virginia.

Crismo's unit made several successful raids on farms and small communities in western Virginia, taking livestock, food, arms, and often filling their pockets with stolen money. In time, the cavalry contingent became little more than a gang of bandits robbing and looting its way across the Appalachian landscape.

One morning the unit was ordered to patrol an area in southwestern Virginia in Tazewell County. The cavalrymen, twenty-four in number, camped on the side of a mountain that overlooked a long, narrow valley. From the signs of agriculture, the valley was rich and productive. At the far end of the valley was a mansion, and the troopers began to consider the prospect of finding something of value there. The farm and the mansion belonged to the wealthy James Grierson.

Anticipating a successful raid with little to no resistance, the cavalrymen rode into the yard, stormed the house, and took Grierson prisoner. They dragged him outside and hung him by the wrists from the limb of a large tree in the front yard. There ensued a lengthy and rather brutal interrogation. Despite being whipped, Grierson steadfastly refused to reveal where his fortune was hidden. It soon became clear to the soldiers that the farmer would rather die than yield his wealth. Frustrated, one of the officers drew his pistol and shot and killed Grierson.

While Grierson was being tortured, John Crismo befriended an old slave. It turned out he was the one who helped the farmer hide his fortune. The slave confessed to Crismo that he knew where the gold coins were buried. At first, the slave refused to show Crismo the location, but subsequent cajoling and a promise of freedom convinced him to cooperate. The slave took Crismo behind the barn, dug about two feet down into the ground, and pulled up one of the heavy sacks of gold coins. Crismo took the sack and warned the slave not to tell any of the other soldiers about the treasure.

Several days later, the cavalry unit was assigned to another location several miles away. After they had arrived at their new destination and established camp, Crismo rode back to the Grierson farm under cover of night and, with the help of the old slave, dug up all of the sacks of gold coins that had been buried behind the barn. The gold was loaded onto some packhorses, which were then led to the location where the cavalry had camped just prior to raiding the Grierson plantation. Several paces from the campground, Crismo and the slave excavated a hole and placed all of the gold coins within, then refilled it and covered it over with rocks and forest debris. On the way back to the farm, Crismo handed the black man several gold coins he had retrieved from one of the sacks and told him to take the money and his family and flee to the North.

Crismo told none of his fellow cavalrymen about the treasure. The following night, Crismo sat by the light of the campfire, withdrew his diary, and sketched a crude map showing the location of the buried coins. Over several pages, he added a description of the terrain and noted certain landmarks. The following day, the cavalry unit left Tazewell County for a new assignment in the eastern part of the state.

As the Civil War raged on, Crismo's regiment engaged in several skirmishes. In one, Crismo was seriously wounded. After a lengthy recovery in a field hospital, he was granted an honorable discharge and sent on his way. At first, Crismo thought about returning to Tazewell County and digging up the gold, but ongoing military action there made it difficult. Crismo gathered his few belongings and traveled westward. He decided to continue his recovery exploring the country. When the war was over, he decided, he would return to the mountain overlooking Grierson's plantation and retrieve the treasure he buried there.

For reasons unexplained, Crismo wandered throughout sparsely settled regions west of the Mississippi River, eventually making his way to Texas. Traveling from town to town and taking odd jobs, the former cavalryman barely made enough to get by. His sparse diary entries during this time suggest that Crismo never entirely recovered from his wound, and that it gave him problems and caused him pain. His writings also suggested that he was not mentally sound.

Years passed, and Crismo landed a job as a cowhand on an isolated ranch several miles out from the town of Pecos, Texas. Though much older than most of the cowhands and quite infirm, Crismo nevertheless proved himself a capable and loyal employee up to the day he passed away in his sleep.

During the months that followed Crismo's death, his diary passed through several hands before winding up in the possession of a Pecos County man who decided to go in search of the buried cache of coins. Following the somewhat vague directions and referring to the clumsily drawn, faded map, the searcher arrived at a small Virginia settlement called Aberdeen. Just north of this hamlet, the man located a narrow valley that had once been part of the Grierson plantation. The land was now state property, having reverted to government ownership after Grierson died leaving no heirs.

A short distance north of the plantation was a prominent mountain, no doubt the one on which Crismo and his cavalry unit camped prior to attacking Grierson's mansion. After exploring the area for several days, the searcher discovered what he deduced must have been an old campsite. Here he found two Union Army canteens, numerous shell casings, and other items suggesting a temporary cavalry bivouac. While Crismo's directions were clear enough to this point, his diary entries never stated on which side of the camp the treasure was buried. For weeks the searcher excavated holes in the area around the old encampment but found nothing. Discouraged, he gave up and went back to Texas.

When he returned home, the searcher placed Crismo's diary on a high dusty shelf in a storeroom where it remained for years. In time, it became lost and no one knows what became of it.

Others, on learning the tale of the buried coin cache on the mountain overlooking Grierson's old plantation, have arrived in the area employing metal detectors and dowsing rods. They have combed the mountains near the old cavalry encampment trying to locate what researchers have suggested is a multimillion-dollar cache, but with no luck.

The treasure, consisting of hundreds of gold coins, remains hidden to this day.

10

THE RED BONE CAVE TREASURE

A lost treasure of gold that has attracted the attention of professional
treasure hunters over many decades is one associated with a location called Red Bone Cave located on the Tennessee River, not far
from Muscle Shoals, Alabama.

A popular legend attributes the origin of this gold to Spanish explorers who arrived in the region under the leadership of Hernando de
Soto. In 1538, King Charles V of Spain provided de Soto with enough
funding to support a company of more than six hundred men. They
were charged with traveling to the New World and, among other
things, to search for precious metals, in particular gold and silver. The
ore was to be processed, cast into ingots, and shipped back to Spain to
fill the country's treasury.

Following a several-month-long voyage across the Atlantic Ocean,
de Soto and his company—soldiers, miners, and priests—traveled, explored, and prospected throughout vast portions of the southern United
States from the east coast of Florida to the Ozark Mountains. According
to very old documents that have since been found in Spanish monaster-
ies, de Soto was successful, for he eventually shipped millions of dollars'
worth of gold and silver back to Spain.

In addition to mining gold, de Soto also acquired quantities of
the ore from several of the Indian villages he encountered during his
explorations. Though the Cherokee did not measure their wealth with
precious metals, they valued gold and silver for fashioning jewelry and
ornaments, which the Spaniard added to the accumulating wealth.
When de Soto observed the abundance of gold the Indians possessed,

he ordered it taken by force. The ornaments were melted down and formed into ingots.

One of the Spanish detachments that had completed a series of successful raids on Cherokee Indian villages was herding a pack train consisting of forty mules laden with gold along a narrow trail through a forested portion of what was to eventually become the state of Alabama. An hour before nightfall, the party came to a village of Chickasaw Indians. During previous encounters, the Chickasaw proved to be friendly, and this occasion was no exception. The encampment was located a few miles south of the Tennessee River along a tributary that provided good, clear water for drinking.

As winter approached, the Chickasaw invited the Spaniards to remain in their village until the cold weather passed. The Spaniards accepted the invitation, enjoying their time with the Indians and helping them hunt for game.

When spring arrived, the Spaniards began to prepare for departure. Their intention was to travel to the southwest and rendezvous with the main part of de Soto's force. Before they left, the leader of the contingent of Spaniards demanded that the chief send one hundred of the tribe's young women to accompany them. The chief refused, and the Spanish grew threatening.

As the Spaniards loaded the gold onto the packhorses, they were surprised by a sudden attack from the now enraged Indians. Panicked, the soldiers mounted their horses and fled from the village. They had no time to finish packing the gold.

The Chickasaw chased the Spaniards northward to the banks of the Tennessee River. The water was high and impossible to cross. With their retreat cut off, the soldiers turned to fight. The battle lasted for almost an hour. When it was over, most of the Spaniards had been killed. The survivors fled into the forest and were never seen again.

When the Chickasaw returned to the village, the chief ordered all of the treasure loaded onto the packhorses and transported north across the river where it would be deposited inside a cave and the entrance sealed.

The ensuing years were good ones for the thriving Chickasaw village. When a white trapper arrived in the area in 1720 to search for beaver in the nearby streams, he first sought permission to do so from the chief of the tribe. Impressed by the young trapper, the chief granted permission and invited him to live in the village while he remained in the area. The trapper chose to do so, and during the following weeks, he and the chief became close friends.

The chief had only one child, a daughter, and as he was very old he grew concerned. He wanted her to find a husband and provide him with grandchildren before he died. The daughter had rejected the courtship of several of the tribe's braves, and the chief was worried that she would never take a mate. The daughter, however, found the young trapper to her liking. Before long the two of them were spending time together.

Late one night about two months after the trapper had come to the village, he was awakened by a pair of Indians. Speaking not a word, they tied his hands behind his back and placed a blindfold over his eyes before he could identify them. The trapper tried to fight them off, but their combined strength was too much for him. As he ceased his struggles, the Indians told him no harm was to come to him if he did what he was told.

For the rest of the night and into the morning of the following day, the trapper was led through the woods. Once, when the group had paused to rest, the trapper could hear the sound of flowing water. A few moments later, the blindfold slipped slightly and he spotted a wide expanse of the Tennessee River before him, along with high limestone bluffs that rose in the distance beyond.

When the Indians were ready to resume their trek, the trapper was placed in a canoe and rowed across the river. Following a brief hike, the three men arrived at a place where the air was cold and the ground damp. The trapper could hear the chirping of bats and realized he was inside a large cave. The three negotiated passages in the cave, then the Indians called a halt. The trapper was untied and the blindfold removed.

In the flickering light of torches carried by the Indians, the trapper looked around a low-ceilinged chamber of a cave. When his eyes adjusted, he recognized the chief of the tribe along with one of the braves. The chief pointed toward the back of the chamber. Hundreds of gold ingots were stacked against the far wall, reaching nearly to the ceiling. Several wooden chests filled with golden jewelry had been placed at the foot of the stack.

After giving the trapper a few minutes to take it all in, the chief told him this place was called Red Bone Cave. He related a tale of the long-ago visiting Spaniards and their conflict with his tribe. The chief also told him that the gold he saw in the chamber was only part of the total amount hidden in the cave.

The chief guided the trapper into another chamber and pointed to several skeletons propped up against a wall. He explained that they were the bones of the warriors that had died during the fight with the fleeing Spaniards. He said the bodies were placed in this cave to guard the treasure against intruders.

The chief stepped up to the trapper, laid a hand upon his shoulder, and told him that all of the treasure in this cave would belong to him if he agreed to marry his daughter and live in the village. If he should chose not to marry the daughter, he would be allowed to leave the village unharmed, but was forbidden to share the location of the treasure cave with anyone.

The tapper considered his options. If he married the daughter, he would be required to live in the village. Possessing the wealth of a king, however, would do him little good, for he would have no opportunity to spend it. Recalling his view of the river and the limestone bluff when the blindfold slipped earlier, the trapper was convinced that he could return to Red Bone Cave on his own and retrieve the treasure for himself.

The trapper explained to the chief that he would like to have a few days to ponder the offer. The chief agreed. The trapper was tied up again, the blindfold reattached, and he was led from the cave and onto the trail back to the village.

It was dark long before the three men returned to the Chickasaw village. Tired from a full day of walking, the chief decided to make camp at a location alongside the trail near a river and spend the night. Three hours before sunrise, the trapper freed himself of his bonds and the blindfold, crept up to the two sleeping Indians, and killed them. This done, he dragged the bodies to the river and threw them in. At dawn, he began the long trek that would take him to Fort Rosalie in the Natchez Territory. He reached his destination several days later.

At the fort, the trapper ran into an old friend. He told him the story of the great treasure lying in the remote cave near the Tennessee River. The friend agreed to accompany him, and the two men spent the next few days preparing to return to Red Bone Cave. Traveling by night and hiding from Indians during the day, the men were weeks on the trail when the trapper's friend wearied of the search and returned to Fort Rosalie.

Now alone, and unable to relocate the cave, the trapper decided to return to the Chickasaw village. At first afraid, the trapper was surprised when he was warmly welcomed by the Indians. He later learned that no one ever knew that the chief and one of the braves had taken him from the village that night a few months earlier. The disappearance of the chief and the warrior remained a mystery to the Chickasaw.

Using the excuse of trapping for furs, the trapper undertook his search for Red Bone Cave. He eventually married the daughter of the chief and lived in the village. Though he searched for Red Bone Cave for years, he was never able to find it

In 1723, the trapper's wife died from fever. He decided to return to Fort Rosalie. On arriving, however, he found the old settlement had long been abandoned. All was in ruins. It had been attacked years earlier by the Natchez Indians, the inhabitants massacred, and all of the buildings burned to the ground.

The trapper took up residence in the abandoned fort and lived there for the rest of his life. During the ensuing years, he made several forays into the wilderness in attempts to relocate Red Bone Cave and the treasure that lay therein, but he never succeeded.

11

THE SILVER BULLETS

Because the price of gold has risen rapidly during the past several decades, over sixteen hundred dollars per ounce at this writing, the attention of miners, prospectors, and treasure hunters has been focused on this precious metal, oftentimes at the expense of others. In recent years, however, the value of silver has increased to the point where it is now high on the list for recovery. One long-lost, and very rich, silver mine located in the Arkansas Ozarks has captured the attention of fortune hunters for over a century

The 1880s and 1890s witnessed significant westward migration from states such as Kentucky, Tennessee, Virginia, and Alabama. Many of the migrants, attracted by the availability of fertile lands on which to undertake agriculture or the possibility of mining gold, headed for the Great Plains or California. Many, however, either from running short of funds or simply wearing of the long days and weeks of travel, settled at the first acceptable place they could find. A number of settlers parked their wagons in the Ozarks of Arkansas, Missouri, and Oklahoma, and set about eking out a living on hardscrabble land that was similar to where they came from in the Appalachians.

Tobe Inmon and his family had been residents of a narrow, poor valley in western Kentucky. They grew some corn on a rocky hillside and raised hogs and chickens in the bottoms and got by. Inmon did not get along well with his neighbors. He earned a reputation as a recluse, neither needing nor wanting the company of others.

When Inmon was accused of stealing a neighbor's livestock and had his life threatened, he decided to pack up the family's meager possessions into a flimsy wagon pulled by two bony horses and head west, driving their hogs ahead of them. They had no notion of a destination, and they wandered aimlessly over poor roads through swamps and forests.

Following a long day of travel in the Ozark Mountains of Arkansas, Inmon realized he had somehow gotten off the main trail and had become lost. As he searched for a way out of the mountains, he arrived at a small valley with a stream of cool, clear water and a flat, fertile floodplain suitable for growing crops. There was plenty of timber on the hillsides for firewood and the construction of a cabin and barn, and there appeared to be adequate forage for his hogs and chickens. There were no neighbors within miles. Tobe Inmon decided he liked the place and told his family this was where they would stay.

Living out of the wagon, Inmon set about the task of building a one-room log cabin and some pens for his hogs. When he found the time, he planted corn and other crops near the creek. Life began to look comparatively good for the Inmons.

The closest settlement to Inmon's valley was the town of Dover, a small settlement lying twelve miles to the north. It was an important stop along the old road to Fort Smith. From time to time, Inmon hauled chickens or a hog into Dover and traded for staples like sugar, salt, coffee, and flour. Here he learned that the location where he resided was called Moccasin Creek Valley. Inmon rarely spoke to anyone in Dover except to conduct a little business. Even then, he was surly, preferring to conclude his affairs and leave as quickly as possible.

Inmon dressed in little more than rags and always appeared unclean and unshaven. The few times he brought his family to town, they too looked wretched and ragged. Those who chanced by Inmon's homestead invariably remarked at the squalor, claiming the log cabin had large open chinks that let in cold air during the winter and appeared to offer little more shelter than the hog pen.

One day in October of 1903, Inmon rode into Dover and asked for a doctor. He explained that his youngest son had come down with a fever and was unconscious. Inmon was taken to Dr. Benjamin Martin, the only physician in town. Martin agreed to follow Inmon out to Moccasin Creek Valley. Martin, an affable man in his late forties, was well liked by everyone in the community, and had delivered practically every child in Dover and the surrounding area under ten years of age. On arriving at the Inmon place, Martin was appalled at the family's destitution, but he agreed to remain at the youth's bedside until the boy was out of danger.

The following day when the fever had passed, Martin harnessed his horse and was preparing his carriage to leave on the return trip to Dover. As the doctor was hitching the animal to the traces, Inmon appeared from around the corner of the barn and asked the fee. Keenly aware of the man's poverty, Martin told Inmon he could settle up when times got better and not to worry about until then. Inmon was insistent, however, and finally offered the doctor a small canvas sack containing about thirty bullets for a large caliber rifle. Inmon told Martin he made them himself.

During this time bullets were scarce. Most people who had need of them were happy to obtain them when they could. Martin examined the bullets closely, found them to be well made, and as he was an enthusiastic hunter and outdoorsman, gratefully accepted them as payment.

As the doctor packed the sack of shells away in the carriage, he asked Inmon how he came by the materials to fashion bullets. Inmon gestured with his thumb toward a nearby ridge and explained that he had made them from lead he dug out of "an old lead mine back yonder in the hills not too far from this place." Martin thanked him again, climbed into his carriage, and returned to Dover.

On arriving at his home, Martin placed the sack of bullets on a shelf in his study. He intended to use them on his next deer hunt. Over the next few weeks, however, the physician stayed busy treating the sick and infirm and delivering babies. As a result, his autumn deer hunt had to be cancelled.

A full two years passed before the doctor remembered the bullets. While readying equipment for a deer hunt, he located the sack of bullets on the shelf and placed them on the desk in his study so that he would not forget to take them along the next morning. That evening while reading at his desk, Martin picked up one of the bullets and turned it over and over in his hand. He scratched at the surface of the bullet, trying to pick off some of the black residue. As a little of the coating was removed, he noted a peculiar color underneath.

On a hunch Martin cancelled his deer hunt. Instead, he traveled to Russellville the next day, a larger settlement several miles south of Dover. There, he took the bullets to a friend knowledgeable about minerals. To his astonishment, the doctor was informed they were made of almost pure silver. Martin sold the sack of shells for seventy-two dollars.

Returning to Dover that evening, Martin made plans to leave for the Inmon homestead at first light. His intention was to try to convince the poor farmer to show him the location of his so-called lead mine.

Martin left at daybreak the following day. So anxious was he to reach the location of the silver mine that he flogged his poor horse the entire trip, his carriage bouncing along the rough and seldom used road until it seemed as though it would come apart.

When Martin drove up to the Inmon cabin he found it deserted. He checked the barn and the pens and discovered that the livestock was also gone. In fact, it appeared as though no one had occupied the site for several months. Martin drove his carriage to the home of the nearest neighbor several miles away and inquired of the whereabouts of the Inmons. He was told that the family packed up everything they owned into their rickety wagon and left for Texas months earlier. They never told anyone where in Texas they were headed.

Martin drove back to the Inmon farm. With only an hour of light left in the day, the physician climbed to the top of a low hill behind the cabin and wandered through the woods. He inspected every rock outcrop he encountered for any evidence of mining. When it became too dark to continue, the doctor made his way down the mountain and returned to Dover. Poor Tobe Inmon, he pondered; the luckless farmer and his family lived little better than the beasts of the forest, and all the while had access to what possibly could have been a significant fortune in silver and didn't know it.

On arriving home, Martin busied himself with preparations for a longer stay at Moccasin Creek Valley in order to properly search for the mine. As he bustled around town purchasing gear and provisions, neighbors remarked that he appeared frantic and was acting strange. Martin refused to offer an explanation for his actions and ignored requests for his medical services. He was, in fact, consumed with the notion of finding the silver mine he was convinced existed somewhere in the hills near Moccasin Creek Valley.

For the next two years, Dr. Martin made forays into that part of the Ozark Mountains in search of what he was convinced would be his fortune. Each trip brought him greater disappointment. Back in Dover, his patients finally gave up on him and sought another doctor for treatment.

Martin continued with his search for the silver mine and eventually ran out of money. He sold his home and practice and used the money to finance his trips to Moccasin Creek Valley. Finding the mine became an all-consuming passion for Martin, and many of his friends in Dover began to believe he had gone insane.

Years passed, and the long and unsuccessful search for Tobe Inmon's lost silver mine left Martin broke, broken, and disheartened. He moved in with a sister who lived in Russellville. His health began to deteriorate rapidly, and not long afterward he died of pneumonia.

On learning the full story of Inmon's silver bullets, a few Dover residents took up the search. During the years following Dr. Martin's death, treasure hunters combed the hills and valleys around Moccasin Creek. On occasion, artifacts were found that were later identified as Spanish mining tools, giving rise to the belief that sometime in the distant past the Spaniards, who were known to have explored the region, may have prospected for, discovered, and mined silver here.

Time passed, and few people arrived at Moccasin Creek Valley to search for the elusive silver. The story was forgotten. Then, several decades later, an incident occurred to rekindle the tale of the lost mine.

In 1951, a Cherokee Indian named Lawrence Mankiller brought a large nugget into Fort Smith where it was identified as a piece of high-grade silver. Mankiller explained that he had found the nugget on the floor of an old mine shaft while hunting for deer near Moccasin Creek Valley. An unexpected rain began to fall, Mankiller explained, and he sought shelter in the convenient shaft. While seated just inside the entrance, he poked around in the rubble on the floor of the shaft and found the nugget. He said there were several more lying near the one he retrieved.

Mankiller received an offer of several hundred dollars from a group of Fort Smith businessmen who wanted him to lead them to the old shaft. Mankiller agreed to the proposition, pocketed the money, and promised to depart for the location the next morning. That night, however, Mankiller disappeared and was never seen in the area again.

Skeptics of the Tobe Inmon tale have suggested that it is all a fabrication, and that silver, along with other precious metals, does not exist in the Ozark Mountains. The skeptics are wrong. Records exist that show that profitable silver mines were operated in the Ozarks in the region of the Buffalo River near the tiny community of Silver Hill, and that small amounts of the ore can still be found there to this day.

The late Piney Page, an Ozark folklorist and chronicler of events, was raised in and around Moccasin Creek Valley. He once told the story of a relative, Grover Page, who, while plowing a cornfield on the floodplain where Moccasin Creek joins Shop Creek, paused in his labors to take a drink from the cool stream. While the young Page was lying on his stomach on the bank sipping water, he spied an object on the bottom that appeared different from the usual gravel. On retrieving it, he found that it was a silver nugget the size of his toe.

The Page family had the nugget assayed, and on the strength of the evaluation, began to explore the creek area for the source of the ore. Some distance up the narrow valley through which runs Shop Creek, a thin seam of silver mixed with lead and zinc was discovered on a west-facing outcrop. The Pages invested in some mining equipment and for several weeks blasted and drilled into the weathered rock in pursuit of the vein of ore. At first, a significant amount of silver was extracted, but as the mining operation progressed, the seam was lost.

Members of the Page family continued to work the mine off and on for the next several years, but the return was not encouraging and they finally gave up and turned their attention back to farming.

Now and then hikers return from Moccasin Creek Valley with samples of rock they collected along the way. Most of the specimens are unremarkable, but once in a while a piece of silver is found among the others, lending even more credence to the notion that the ore can be found in the area. Eventually some hiker or hunter making his or her way through the woods in the region may stumble upon Tobe Inmon's old mine shaft. If one of them is able to recognize silver in its natural state, that individual may have found the lost mine that has eluded so many for so long.

12

THE LOST GOLD
MINE OF THE COSSATOT

Southwestern Arkansas is a land of remote hollows and dark places. This region teems with tales of ghosts and spirits, of bandits and hermits, and of lost treasure. The Cossatot River flows out of the Ouachita Mountains here. In its upper reaches it is swift and violent, a challenge to kayakers and canoeists. The name comes from an Indian word that means "skull-crusher."

Over geologic time, the Cossatot has relentlessly carved through overlying layers of sandstone and shale that make up the greater portion of the mountains. Here and there, the underlying granite is exposed, rock formed during a bygone era when belowground volcanic activity dominated the region. In Sevier County, the Cossatot River eroded away a significant amount of overlying rock and exposed intrusive granite along with an accompanying seam of gold. This vein was apparently discovered by Spanish explorers under the command of de Soto, men who entered the area centuries ago in search of riches. They mined the gold, eventually digging a vertical shaft that extended over one hundred feet. For whatever reason, the Spaniards abandoned the area while the mine was still productive. It was later found by early settlers and then lost again.

During the late 1860s, Dr. Ferdinand Smith drove his family and belongings in a wagon from Frankford, Missouri, to the remote and sparsely settled country of Sevier County along the Cossatot River. Some had written that Smith was looking for a piece of land to farm. Others maintained he was driven from Missouri as a result of the mysterious deaths of some of his patients. Whatever the circumstances, none of this information was known to the few residents of Sevier County, all of whom welcomed the physician. Up until then, they had no access to a doctor and treated their ailments with folk remedies and potions. Smith became popular in a short time, making himself available to the sick and injured, and accepting payment in livestock and produce.

Dr. Smith had an interest in history, and before long he was soliciting information on what people knew of the area, its earliest settlers, and the Indians who passed through the region from time to time. In this manner, Smith learned a fascinating tale of a lost gold mine located some distance upstream of his farm on the Cossatot River. Eventually, Smith learned even more details of the lost mine from Choctaw Indians who had settled in the Cossatot area.

Several years before the Choctaws moved to the region, a trading post had been established at the site known today as Lockesburg. The post stocked food, tools, clothing, guns, and ammunition, most of which was exchanged for pelts. The post also served as a gathering place for local trappers and hunters.

Once a month, a blond, fair-skinned woman arrived at the post on a white horse, accompanied by four young Indians. The woman was described as being clothed in garments of leather and adorned in gold jewelry of rustic design and manufacture. She would purchase foodstuffs and other items, all of which she paid for with gold. The nuggets were described as being of a remarkably high quality. On the few occasions the woman spoke, it was in Spanish. When asked how she had come by the gold she refused to answer. Her Indian companions also remained mute to such questions. Several attempts were made to follow her after her visits to the trading post, but she always managed to elude her trackers.

Now and then someone would encounter the woman and her companions returning from the trading post along the trail that has since become known as the Old Fort Towson Road. Following one particular trip to the post, she was seen entering Pig Pen Bottoms, a snake and wild hog–infested patch of briars in the dark woods on the floodplain of the Cossatot River. When the observer told friends at the trading post what he had seen, a small expedition was organized to enter the bottoms in search of the source of the woman's gold.

The party had a difficult time finding a way into the forbidding area. Once there, they became lost, wandering for hours before making their way out. One man suffered a bite from a water moccasin. They finally returned to the trading post around midnight, exhausted, scratched, and unsuccessful. The incident apparently put the strange woman on guard, for she was never seen again.

In time, Dr. Smith purchased a parcel of land south of Rolling Shoals Ford on the Cossatot River. Pig Pen Bottoms was located between the ford and Smith's land. The large, dense thicket appeared impenetrable and resisted all of Smith's attempts to enter. Undaunted, he hired a group of men to clear the area so it could be placed into production. When most of the tangle of briers and vines had been cut and burned, an entrance to an old mine shaft was discovered in an outcropping of rock. The shaft was nearly vertical. Judging from the piles of rock adjacent to the entrance, it had been extensively worked. Peering into the shaft, Smith spotted several old, rotting timbers that served as bracing. Smith, along with several of his employees, attempted to enter the shaft, but it was almost entirely filled with water.

According to Smith, there was no recollection among the older residents of the area of any mining in the bottoms. On the other hand, history records that Spanish explorers under de Soto visited the region in search of gold and silver. The evidence suggests that they found some.

For several years the shaft remained inaccessible because of the standing water. Smith could only dream of the riches that might lie at its deepest recesses, and he pondered ways to obtain them. Before he was able to enter the mine, Dr. Smith passed away, his hopes of retrieving gold from the old mine unfulfilled.

During the early 1920s, a severe drought struck the area. The Cossatot River dried to a mere trickle. Wells went dry as the water table throughout that part of Arkansas dropped. Around this time, someone noticed that the water level in the old Spanish mine in Pig Pen Bottoms had receded. A group of men decided to make an attempt at entering the shaft.

Using ropes, two men were lowered into the mine. Each carried a lantern and a shovel. As they descended into the mine, they noticed rotting timbers all the way down that had once served as mine supports.

Undoubtedly, a considerable amount of work had gone into the excavation of the shaft. During his descent, one of the men found a large,
heavy hammer that had been lodged between the wall of the shaft and
a timber support. It was later identified as having been cast in the town
of Seville, Spain, during the early part of the sixteenth century, thus
providing greater evidence of the presence of Spaniards there.

At nearly one hundred feet into the shaft, the two men encountered water and were forced to return to the surface. Following two
more descents into the mine, it was determined that it would be impossible to reach the bottom unless the water could be removed. In early
1927, another drought struck the region, and the water table was even
lower than it had been during the earlier dry spell. Yet another group
of men familiar with the tale of the lost gold mine made plans for a descent. This time when they reached the bottom at 120 feet, there was
no water. They did, however, encounter a deep layer of sediment that
had been deposited, sand and silt undoubtedly carried into the mine by
floodwaters during previous years. Believing the sediment was far too
deep to penetrate in order to reach the vein of gold, they abandoned
the project. Thus, the deepest recesses of the shaft remained unexplored.

The drought continued, getting worse with each passing week. A
group of boys who had heard the story of the lost Spanish gold mine
decided to make an attempt to reach the bottom of the shaft. After de-
scending 120 feet into the mine, they encountered the deep layer of silt.

For days, the boys labored to remove the silt, hauling bucket loads
to the surface at every opportunity. As they carried the fill to the surface
and worked their way deeper into the shaft, they noticed that it grew
narrower, suggesting they were nearing the vein of gold. By this time
they had excavated several tons of dirt. In the process they found more
old Spanish mining tools, thus fueling their optimism that a fortune in
gold was near at hand.

Then the rain began to fall. The excavation of the shaft was halted
as the boys were forced to wait out the weather. Luck was not with
them, however, for the rains did not abate for days. In fact, it was the
beginning of a series of thunderstorms that struck most of the state of
Arkansas that year, eventually giving rise to the Great Flood of 1927
that placed much of Arkansas and Louisiana underwater. The Cossatot
River, carrying a heavy burden of sand and silt, rose and overflowed

its banks, spilling over into the floodplain where the mine was located. Crops were ruined, but the farmers tried to content themselves with the notion that the fresh deposits along the floodplain would result in a more fertile bottomland. They were already planning for next year's planting.

When the rains finally abated and the floodwaters retreated, the boys returned to Pig Pen Bottoms to evaluate the status of the digging operation. The flood deposits obliterated all traces of the shaft, and it was only after several years of searching that the entrance was finally found again, located beneath two feet of alluvial deposit.

During successive years, several parties attempted to re-excavate the sediment-filled shaft, but none were successful. Water in the shaft remained the ongoing problem. No sooner would some progress be attained relative to removing the tons of silt than the spring rains would arrive, bringing more floodwaters. In addition, for years the local water table had been rising, causing the shaft to fill to within a few feet of the surface. All attempts at pumping the water out failed.

Today, the old Spanish gold mine lies undisturbed in Pig Pen Bottoms. Though the regrowth of briars and brush has partially concealed the location, a few residents of nearby Gilliam, Arkansas, claim to know where it is. There is little interest among them relative to making another attempt at digging into the shaft. They have seen and heard too much about the difficulties of previous attempts. They are also familiar with the unpredictability of the Cossatot River.

Most of them are convinced that a fortune in gold remains at the bottom of the old mine. Some are optimistic that it can be reached using modern methods. Others, however, are certain that no one will ever get to the gold because the forces of nature will conspire to foil their quest.

13

THE LOST TREASURE
OF SKELETON CANYON

During the latter part of the nineteenth century, a gang of Arizona and New Mexico based bandits organized a raid on the city of Monterrey in the Mexican state of Nuevo Leon. While robbing the bank and sacking the town's church, the robbers were confronted by a small contingent of Mexican soldiers and police and a battle ensured, during which several of the soldiers were killed.

Packing their booty consisting of gold and silver coins, diamonds, and golden crucifixes, chalices, and other valuable religious artifacts onto a number of stout mules, the outlaws fled Monterrey, heading northwest toward a remote and seldom-used pass through the mountains far to the northwest and near a point where Mexico, New Mexico, and Arizona share a common boundary.

At the time of the robbery, it was estimated that the value of the loot exceeded two million dollars. It consisted of one million dollars' worth of diamonds, thirty-nine bars of gold, dozens of bags of gold and silver coins, and an undetermined amount of gold statuary taken from the church. The journey from Monterrey to the pass was almost a thousand miles long, wandering over poor roads and trails. The outlaws were pursued for several days, but the soldiers were no match for their weaponry and marksmanship. Eventually, they abandoned the pursuit and returned to Monterrey.

Weeks later when the party crossed the international border in southeastern Arizona, they wound their way through a little-known canyon. Here, intrigue and double cross led to an ambush that resulted in the deaths of at least a dozen men and the burial of a substantial portion of the treasure. Since then, the pass has been known as Skeleton Canyon.

In 1891, a small gang of bandits led by a man believed to be the notorious outlaw Curly Bill Brocious terrorized stagecoach shipments and travelers in the vicinity of Silver City, New Mexico. According to some researchers, Brocious was killed by Wyatt Earp during a gun battle near Tombstone. The claim is based almost entirely on a statement by Earp. However, Brocious's body was never found. According to some, the outlaw fled to New Mexico where he continued his life of crime holding up stagecoaches.

For months, Brocious and his gang plied their outlaw trade, but by the time the spoils of the robberies were divided by the five men, the rewards were slim. Curly Bill wanted to move on to bigger, more lucrative targets, but remained unsure how to go about it.

One evening the five outlaws met at Brocious's cabin located not far from Silver City. The gang members included Jim Hughes, Zwing Hunt, Billy Grounds, and Doc Neal. Several years earlier, Hughes had killed three people during a stagecoach robbery in Texas. He was nearly caught by law enforcement authorities but succeeded in escaping across the border into Mexico. He fled to Monterrey, where he lived for a year. During his time there he grew proficient in Spanish and also learned of various riches found in that city.

When Hughes decided to leave Monterrey, he traveled westward, ending up in the Mexican state of Sonora. Here he fell in with José Estrada, a feared Mexican bandit and killer. Hughes proved to be a competent and fearless member of the gang, one of thirty to forty members, and he remained with the bandit leader for several months. Following a series of raids, the Estrada gang was pursued by a Mexican army patrol, forcing them to take refuge in the Sierra Madres close to the border of the United States. At this point, Hughes bade his friend Estrada goodbye and told him he was going to head back toward home. A short time later, he joined Curly Bill's gang in Silver City.

While Hughes was meeting with Brocious and the other outlaws that evening, he related stories of his time in Mexico, and in particular, Monterrey. Intrigued, Brocious suggested they travel to that city and raid it. The other outlaws agreed, eager for the wealth they knew they would realize from such an escapade.

Hughes thought the idea good, but explained that a gang of Anglos riding into Monterrey would arouse suspicion. Besides, he said, five men were not enough. They needed a small army. Then he offered an idea. He would contact his friend Estrada and enlist his aid in conducting the robbery. He would explain to Estrada that disposing of the loot in Mexico would be a problem, and that if he transported it to the United States, he and Brocious would arrange for its exchange, converting the gold and gems into cash and making him and his gang members all rich men. Hughes had a plan, and it involved double-crossing the greedy Estrada.

Hughes said he would accompany Estrada and his men to Monterrey. After the raid, he would then lead them back to the United States to a specific location. Once Estrada's gang and all of the loot were within the confines of the canyon east of Sloan's Ranch, explained Hughes, Brocious and his gang would ambush them and take the treasure. Hughes's plan appealed to the gang members and they agreed to send their companion into Sonora to find Estrada and explain the proposal.

After weeks of planning and travel, the raid was ready to be launched. Telegraph wires were cut, and mules were procured to transport the booty. The bank and church were sacked. Much to the surprise of the bandits, a fortune in cut diamonds was found in the bank vault. During the raid, four Monterrey police officers were shot and killed, along with at least a dozen soldiers. Three hours later, the bandits rode out of town with gold and silver bars and coins, priceless golden statuary from the church, and diamonds. The booty was packed into sacks and saddlebags and lashed to the mules.

The outlaws fled due west, following the wagon road to Torreon. Occasional firefights erupted with their pursuers, who eventually turned back. Near Torreon, the party turned northward and made their way along a snaking road through the Sierra Madres that eventually took them to an old smuggler's trail that led into Arizona.

Once across the border, the weary bandits made camp in a narrow canyon near the confluence of what are now Skeleton Creek and the South Fork of Skeleton Creek. By this time, most of Estrada's gang members had been paid off and sent home. The treasure was now guarded by the Mexican bandit leader himself along with a dozen handpicked men. Hughes told Estrada he was going to ride ahead and make the arrangements for the transfer of the treasure and would return in a few days.

Several days later, Hughes returned to the canyon with Grounds, Hunt, and Neal. For reasons not clear, Brocious remained in Silver City. Early one morning, Hughes led his partners to a point about two miles north of Estrada's camp where they set up an ambush. At this point, the canyon was so narrow that the mules and riders would have to pass through single file. The Mexicans would be easy targets. When his men were positioned for the assault, Hughes told them to open fire at his signal, which would be a pistol shot. Then he rode back to Estrada's camp.

Hours later, Estrada's men loaded the treasure onto the mules and doused the campfires. The riders mounted and prepared for travel. Hughes told Estrada they were to ride to Silver City where the treasure would be exchanged for cash. Following the transfer, there would be a celebration. It was late afternoon by the time the treasure caravan entered the narrow part of the canyon. Hughes was in the lead, with Estrada riding behind him.

When the line of riders and pack animals was strung out in the narrow defile, Hughes turned in his saddle and shot Estrada in the head. At this, Grounds, Hunt, and Neal opened fire with their rifles, and within seconds, all of the Mexicans were dead.

During the slaughter, the pack mules carrying a portion of the treasure panicked and bolted. Unable to overtake and control them, the riders decided that the only way to stop them was to shoot them. All save two were downed before they could escape the canyon. One was shot just outside of the canyon entrance and the last was finally overtaken miles away near Geronimo's Peak.

With the killing of the mules a problem arose. Now there was no way to transport the greatest portion of the Monterrey loot to the designated hiding place. Neal volunteered to ride to Silver City and secure more mules. Grounds and Hunt were to remain in the canyon to guard the treasure. While discussion ensued, Hunt asked why Brocious was to get a share of the treasure when he did nothing to help obtain it. Eventually, it was decided to leave Curly Bill out of the split. Hughes would ride back to Silver City and tell Brocious that Estrada escaped with all of the treasure. If Brocious acted suspicious, Hughes was to kill him. Hughes would then return to Skeleton Canyon with the necessary mules where he, Grounds, Neal, and Hunt would load the treasure and transport it to some safe location.

Within hours after Hughes rode away, Grounds, Hunt, and Neal decided to keep the treasure for themselves. With Brocious and Hughes nowhere around, they could divide the fortune three ways, each of them receiving a greater share than under the previous plan. Doc Neal was elected to travel to a nearby ranch and purchase some oxen to carry the treasure. Taking a pocketful of the gold coins, he rode away while Grounds and Hunt set up camp.

Once Neal was out of sight, Grounds and Hunt gathered up the treasure that had been carried by the mules, excavated a deep hole not far from the campsite and about one mile from the massacre site, and buried most of it. According to some estimates, the two men buried, in 1890s values, approximately eighty thousand dollars' worth of the loot. Some researchers quibble with this figure, claiming it could be as much as one million dollars or more.

Neal rode into camp two days later, leading four oxen roped together. It did not take him long to realize he had been double-crossed by his two partners. He noted that several of the leather pouches containing the treasure lay open and empty and several of the mule packs were missing. He said nothing, fearing that revealing his suspicions might get him killed. The following morning, the three men loaded the remaining treasure onto the oxen.

For the next two days, the outlaws herded the oxen northeastward toward New Mexico. Then, just before reaching the border, they turned northward into the Peloncillo Mountains. As they rode along, Neal noted that Grounds and Hunt often rode close together and spoke in whispers. Neal was convinced the two men intended to kill him. At the first opportunity, he broke away from the pack train and fled eastward. He later reported that Grounds and Hunt fired their rifles at him as he fled, but he was not struck.

Neal rode straight for Silver City. Here he discovered Brocious had been arrested for fighting and was in the jailhouse. Hughes was living in the outlaw's cabin. Hughes had not seen Brocious since his return and had been unable to tell him the concocted story of Estrada's escape with the treasure. When Neal told Hughes all that had transpired after he left, he grew angry. The two men decided that when Brocious was released from jail, the three of them would go after Grounds and Hunt.

When Brocious was finally released from jail, Hughes and Neal took him to a saloon where they explained what had occurred. On learning of the deception, Brocious grew livid. At some point, a young barmaid banged into his chair and the volatile Brocious, losing control, pulled his revolver and shot her dead. Realizing they were facing serious charges, the three men fled Silver City with a posse on their heels.

Some forty miles later, the posse caught up with and cornered the three outlaws at the little town of Shakespeare to the southwest. During the gunfight that ensued, Neal was killed. Brocious and Hughes were forced to surrender and within hours were hanged in the dining room of Shakespeare's Pioneer Hotel.

By the time Brocious and Hughes were dangling from the rafters of the Pioneer, Hunt and Grounds, after filling their pockets with gold coins from the hoard, had buried the remainder of the treasure in a canyon running out of Davis Mountain near Morenci, Arizona. Then they moved to Tombstone.

Within weeks, word of the massacre of the Estrada gang in what was now being called Skeleton Canyon circulated throughout that part of the Southwest, but no one save Grounds and Hunt knew the circumstances. While maintaining their secret, the two men spent gold recklessly in Tombstone.

Grounds remembered a former girlfriend living in Charleston, a small town not far from Tombstone, and he went to see her. Since Grounds had left months earlier, she had taken up with the Charleston butcher. When Grounds arrived and showed her all of his gold coins, she decided to go back to him. One night as they were lying together in bed, he told her the story of the Monterrey raid, the treasure, and the incident in Skeleton Canyon.

The next morning after Grounds returned to Tombstone, the woman told the butcher what she had learned. The butcher rode to

Tombstone to inform Sheriff Bill Breckenridge of the two murderers, Grounds and Hunt, living in his town. While the butcher was talking to Breckenridge, Grounds had returned to Charleston. The girlfriend immediately confessed to him what she had done. Panicked, Grounds rode his horse at a hard gallop back to Tombstone, told Hunt what had happened, and the two fled.

Before leaving, Grounds took a few minutes to write a letter to his mother who was living in San Antonio, Texas. In the letter, Grounds told her he was coming home, that he was tired of this "wild life." He wrote that he had buried eighty thousand dollars that "I came by honestly." He said he intended to purchase a ranch near San Antonio where his mother could live out her days. Enclosed with the letter was a map showing the location of the treasure buried in Skeleton Canyon.

There was no immediate pursuit of Grounds and Hunt, and they spent the night at a ranch owned by a man named Chandler located about ten miles from Tombstone. The next morning, however, the two outlaws were awakened by Sheriff Breckenridge, who called for them to come out of the bunkhouse with their hands up. Breckenridge, accompanied by two deputies named Gillespie and Young, had followed Grounds and Hunt from Tombstone.

Not wishing to be captured, Grounds and Hunt ran out of the bunkhouse firing their guns. Gillespie was killed immediately, and Young was incapacitated with a bullet in his leg. Breckenridge raised his shotgun and discharged it, the pellets striking Grounds in the head. Dropping the shotgun, the sheriff pulled his revolver and shot Hunt through the chest, inflicting a debilitating wound. The two wounded outlaws were tossed into a buckboard appropriated from rancher Chandler and transported back to Tombstone. Grounds died before arriving, and Hunt was admitted to the local hospital. On first examination, the doctor gave him no chance to live.

Hunt lingered on, requesting authorities to contact his brother Hugh. Days later, Hugh arrived from Tucson. The two visited for only a few minutes, then Hugh left. That afternoon, he leased a horse and buggy, clandestinely removed Zwing Hunt from the hospital, and drove out of town. The escape was not discovered until the next day.

On a hunch, Sheriff Breckenridge decided the Hunt brothers were headed to Skeleton Canyon to dig up the treasure. He gathered a couple of deputies and rode in that direction. Several miles from the massacre site, he encountered a freshly dug grave next to an oak tree. On the trunk of the tree, the name Zwing Hunt was carved. Breckenridge ordered his deputies to dig up the grave. Inside they found Hunt's body. They reburied it and returned to Tombstone. The posse searched the area for hours but encountered no evidence of any digging.

By now, all of the participants in the caching of the Monterrey loot were dead.

The letter and map that Grounds sent to his mother in San Antonio are still in the possession of his descendants. They are reported to be in good condition, and the map supposedly provides clear directions to the location of the buried treasure. To date, and for reasons unknown, no attempt has been made by the Grounds family to recover the buried treasure in Skeleton Canyon.

Over the years, many have gone in search of the buried Monterrey loot, now popularly known as the Skeleton Canyon Treasure. In Skeleton Canyon, dozens, perhaps hundreds, of gold and silver coins have been found, likely those scattered by the pack mules while attempting to flee the site of the massacre. It has been written that just before he died, Zwing Hunt wrote a description of the burial site of the remainder of the treasure that was carried away on the oxen. He stated that it was cached in a canyon near the Davis Mountains. Many consider the directions worthless since there are no Davis Mountains in the area.

It is important to remember, however, that when Grounds and Hunt herded the treasure-laden oxen north after Neal rode away, they traveled for a few more days, turning north near the Arizona–New Mexico border. Conceivably, they could have reached the area of Morenci, Arizona. Just a short distance north of Morenci is a Davis Mountain.

✥

The treasure buried in Skeleton Canyon has never been found. If located today, according to experts, the value could amount to more than twenty million dollars. Further, the remainder of the treasure buried in a canyon associated with Davis Mountain near Morenci has never been found, although in 1995 a man exploring in the area encountered evidence of a curious excavation. He also found the remains of oxen buried nearby. He revealed his discovery to two others but provided no precise directions to the location. Before he was able to excavate for the treasure, he passed away, and the location remains unknown.

14

THE LOST YOACHUM DOLLARS

An Ozark Mystery

America's Ozark Mountains provide an abundance of lore and leg-end: ghosts, monsters, folk wisdom, and tales of lost mines and buried treasures. One of the most enduring, and tantalizing, legends to come from this fascinating mountain range is the one associated with the lost Yoachum silver dollars. There is no doubt that these dollars existed, hundreds of them. Government records substantiate their presence and use during the mid-nineteenth century and collectors possess examples of them. The origin of the silver used in the manufacture of these coins, however, is still being debated. The mysterious cave where the silver was allegedly found is searched for today, as are hundreds, perhaps thousands, more of the coins.

✦

This strange tale has its origins in 1541. In that year, Spanish explorers under the leadership of Hernando de Soto arrived in the remote, iso-lated, and rugged valleys of the Ozark Mountains in search of precious metals. Their goal was to find gold and silver, extract, smelt, and ship it back to the treasuries in Spain.

One of de Soto's prospecting parties explored a portion of the Ozark Mountain country in southwestern Missouri. Ore was found, and a preliminary survey was promising enough to encourage the Span-iards to establish a small settlement in the area while the mines were developed. Atop Bread Tray Mountain, located near the junction of the White and James Rivers and three miles northwest of the present-day town of Lampe, Missouri, they constructed a fortress, the remains of which can still be seen.

While construction of the fortification was under way, a nearby shaft was found. In some accounts it has been described as a cave, but this is unlikely. Most conclude the low, narrow opening was the result of some small-scale and occasional mining by the Indians. Inside the shaft, a thick vein of silver was discovered. In short order, the Spaniards captured and enslaved a number of local Indians and put them to work in the mine digging out the silver. Within weeks, a forty-foot-long shaft had been excavated following the vein of silver. The ore was processed into eighteen-inch-long ingots. As the ingots accumulated, they were stacked against one side of the passageways until they could be packed onto mules and transported to a location on the Mississippi River. From there, the silver was to be floated to the port on the Gulf of Mexico where it would be loaded onto a ship bound for Spain.

The Indians were treated cruelly by the Spaniards. They were whipped, fed poor rations, and chained together at night so they could not escape. From time to time, guards reported that the activities of the Spaniards were being observed by other Indians watching from the nearby ridge tops. Fearing attack, the Spaniards doubled their guards.

When the Spaniards ran low of fresh meat, hunting parties were sent out to bring down deer, turkey, and other game. During these times, the hunting parties often ran into Indians and confrontation ensued. On several occasions, the hunters never returned. Increasingly, the Spaniards grew more wary of and nervous about the attacks and discussed the possibility of loading what silver they had processed and abandoning the area.

Early one morning as the Spaniards were finishing breakfast, hundreds of Indians surged out of the adjacent woods and attacked them, killing all but a handful. At the mine, all of the overseers were slain and the captive Indians released. During the melee, a few of the Spaniards escaped. The silver that had been accumulated was left in the cavern. With the Spaniards gone and the Indians returned to their villages, the cave remained undisturbed for two and a half centuries.

In 1809, a small hunting party of Choctaw Indians got caught in a violent spring thunderstorm and sought refuge in the mine shaft. While waiting for the storm to abate, they explored passageways in the mine and discovered the stacks of silver ingots. They also found several skeletons, most likely the remains of some of the Spaniards as a result of the attack 250 years earlier. The Choctaw, like most Indians, had little use for the ore save for the occasional ornament. Through increased contact with trappers and traders, however, they learned that they could trade the shiny metal for horses, guns, ammunition, and blankets. When the rain let up, the Indians conducted a two-day ceremony at the entrance of the cave designed to rid the place of evil spirits.

For years thereafter, the Choctaw made annual trips to the cave to retrieve enough silver to conduct trade and make a bit of jewelry. They carried the silver as far east as St. Louis, Missouri, to barter for goods.

One afternoon, a Choctaw scout reported that a party of Mexicans was riding toward the cave along a trail that paralleled the White River. The leader of the Indians, accompanied by three armed warriors, rode out to meet the newcomers and requested an explanation for their presence in the Indian homeland.

The Mexicans explained that they were searching for a silver mine that had been discovered and worked by their countrymen many generations earlier. One of the Mexicans unrolled a large sheepskin map replete with Spanish markings and symbols. The Choctaw chief recognized several landmarks indicated on the map. Concerned about the presence of the strangers in Choctaw territory, the chief said there was no such mine and told them to leave.

After the Mexicans rode away, the Choctaw were concerned that the strangers might return and find the silver mine, so the chief ordered that the entrance be sealed and the region abandoned until he deemed it safe to return. The cave remained closed until many years later when other Indians arrived in the valley.

Following the War of 1812, the Delaware Indians, originally from Ohio, Indiana, and Illinois, were relocated into the Ozark Mountains. New white settlers and their accompanying politics caused these Indians to be evicted from their native homelands and sent to a destination that landed most of them in the James River area of the Missouri Ozark by 1820. Here, they mingled with other tribes: Kickapoo, Shawnee, Potowatami, and Seneca, all likewise chased from their traditional lands in the east.

Around this same time, the Yoachum family moved into the James River valley and established a farm. The name has been found throughout the American South and Appalachians and has been subjected to numerous spellings: Yocum, Yokum, Joachim, Yoakum, Yochum, and Yoachum. Most researchers believe the members of the clan who moved to the James River area spelled it Yoachum.

James Yoachum, the patriarch of the James River Yoachums, was born in Kentucky around 1772. One year later, a brother, Solomon, was born. Two years later, a third brother, whose name is unknown, arrived. While the boys were young, the family moved to Illinois, where they established a farm. James, however, had a wanderlust and was not content with the tedium of farm labor. On the day he turned eighteen, he left home, deciding to travel to Missouri to pursue the life of a trapper in the Ozark Mountains in the southwestern part of the state.

James experienced some impressive successes as a trapper, so much so that he decided to return to Illinois and try to talk his brothers into joining him in his enterprise. When he arrived at the family home, he learned that his wife had died in childbirth, leaving him with a son. The boy, Jacob Levi, was being raised by Solomon and his wife.

James remained on the farm for several years but never took to the drudgery of manual labor. When he could stand it no longer, he informed the family that he was returning to the Ozark Mountains to resume his trapping operation. His two brothers, along with his son, agreed to join him within a few months.

On returning to the Missouri Ozarks, James met and married a Delaware Indian woman named Winona and built a small cabin near the confluence of the James and White Rivers. Some historians claim that the James River was named for James Yoachum as a result of the prominent and productive farm he established in the area.

As a result of a number of logistical difficulties, the brothers' move to the Ozarks was delayed and they did not arrive until 1815. By this time, James had planted a large portion of the floodplain in corn and squash and was raising fine herds of cattle and horses. Most of James's neighbors were Delaware Indians. The Delawares tended to be a peaceable tribe and often brought gifts of food to new settlers. In return, James shared a portion of his harvest with his new friends. Occasionally, he gifted a horse to a selected member of the tribe.

While living among the Delaware, James noticed that many of them wore jewelry and ornaments fashioned from silver. When he inquired about the origin of the ore, the Indians told him that many years earlier an aged Choctaw had told them of the existence of a huge fortune in silver ingots stacked shoulder-high in a remote cave deep in the Ozark forest. From another Indian, James learned the story of the Spaniards' visit and the development of the silver mine. When James asked about the location of the cave, he was informed that the Choctaw and the Delaware Indians made a pact never to reveal it to anyone.

Respecting the agreement made by the Indians, James never broached the subject again. Years passed, and the federal government initiated an Indian removal process wherein many of the tribes were evicted from their homelands and resettled on reservations in what was called Indian Territory (now Oklahoma). The new resettlement guidelines affected James's neighbors, the Delaware.

As the tribe was packing their belongings and preparing to leave the area, James and his brothers arrived to assist. They brought along gifts for their friends, including blankets, cooking utensils, and horses. In gratitude, several of the Delaware leaders, after conferring among themselves, agreed to show the Yoachums the location of the secret silver cave. Within days after the departure of the Indians, the brothers located the cave. As with the Indians, the three brothers agreed among themselves never to share the information with anyone. With one exception, the Yoachums apparently carried the secret to their graves.

Whenever the Yoachums needed silver, they went to the cave and retrieved it. The trip from the farm would take two to three days. When they returned with a few ingots, they told their wives that they were taken from a stack of hundreds found along one wall of the cave. Over time, the brothers accumulated an impressive pile of the ingots.

In time more and more settlers arrived in that part of the Ozarks and more and more trading posts were established. As the Yoachums became deeply involved in the commerce of the day, they found opportunities to do business with the new settlers and the new establishments.

The largest business in the area was named the James Fork Trading Post. It was owned by the business firm of Menard and Valle, who had headquarters in St. Genevieve, Missouri, and managed by a man named William Gillis. Even though the Yoachums had one of the most productive farms in the area and a fine market for their produce, they continued to hunt and trap. They traded their furs at the James Fork enterprises for coffee, sugar, flour, and other staples.

Trading Post co-owner Colonel Pierre Menard was a longtime friend of the Indians in the area and dealt with them fairly. Being a Frenchman, he was also very protective of the French trappers in the region and considered the Yoachums outsiders. As a result, the Yoachums were denied credit at the trading post and were made to pay cash—federally issued gold or silver coins—for their purchases. The Yoachums, though rich in silver, had no money.

To remedy the situation, the brothers, led by James, decided to make their own money. Employing simple blacksmith tools, they made dies, melted down the ingots, rolled the silver out into sheets, and stamped out their own coins. On one side, the coins bore the inscription "Yoachum" and the date "1822." The other side was stamped "United States of America" and "1 Dollar."

Over a period of several months, the Yoachums produced thousands of these coins and placed a number of them into circulation. Before long, most of the residents of that part of the Ozark Mountains were using the Yoachum dollars for all of their business transactions. At the trading post, Gillis, after examining the coins and judging them to be made from almost pure silver, accepted them as a legitimate medium of exchange. In a short time, the Yoachum dollars became more common in the remote Ozarks than government-issued money.

This worked well for several years. Outside of this remote and relatively inaccessible region, no one heard of the Yoachum dollars. Residents in the area, however, were content with the way things were going.

In 1845, the Yoachum dollars were brought to the notice of the federal government. When the former Indian lands in the region of the James and White Rivers were opened for purchase by non-Indians, the feds sent a surveying crew to establish section lines and county boundaries. Around this time, the settlers in the area were notified that they would now be required to abide by certain laws relative to securing proper titles to the property on which they lived. Part of the requirement was to pay a filing fee at the government office in Springfield.

Intent on paying their filing fee, dozens of James River residents, along with others in the region, arrived at the government office in Springfield and tried to pay with Yoachum silver dollars.

The agent on duty refused to accept the coins, citing an 1833 regulation that required federally issued coin. He informed the settlers that unless they paid in legitimate United States money, they would not be granted official titles to their land.

Enraged, as well as weary from the long journey into Springfield, several of the men pointed loaded rifles at the agent and told him that the Yoachum coins meant more to the residents in the area than government money and that he had better accept it or suffer the consequences. In fear for his life, the agent accepted the Yoachum dollars and presented each person a valid certificate for his land.

The agent lost no time in informing authorities in Washington, D.C. He also sent along the Yoachum dollars he had collected. When the coins arrived, they were examined and found to contain more silver than the government issued silver dollar.

The federal authorities did not classify the Yoachum dollars counterfeit because there was no attempt to duplicate government-minted coins. They were more concerned about the proliferation of nonfederal money in the region. The nation's coin and currency decision makers wired the Springfield office and ordered the agent to confiscate Yoachum dollars and determine the location of the silver mine.

A few weeks after receiving his orders, the agent arrived at James Yoachum's house and informed him that he was there to take a look at the silver mine. James pointed a rifle at the agent and ordered him off of his property. Intimidated, the agent hurried away, but returned one week later with a contingent of eight other federal agents, all armed and trying their best to look menacing. On this occasion, the agent explained to James the official position of the U.S. government relative to the renegade silver dollars and informed Yoachum that he was officially discouraged from manufacturing and distributing any more of the coins.

James Yoachum was generally considered a law–abiding and patriotic citizen. He told the agents that he never willfully intended to break any laws. He agreed to cease making the dollars but refused to reveal the location of the silver mine. Discussions continued into the evening with both parties refusing to budge from their positions. The stalemate was finally broken when the agent agreed to not prosecute the Yoachum brothers if they agreed to halt manufacture of the coins. The location of the old Spanish mine was to remain a secret.

A few more years passed, and in 1848 James Yoachum died. One version of his demise states that he was taken down with fever and died in his sleep. Another version is that he and his wife, Winona, were killed in a cave-in at the mine during a trip to retrieve some the silver.

Following James's death, the two brothers decided to abandon the Ozarks and travel to California. The gold fields were just opening up and the brothers wanted to try their luck at prospecting for gold. Just before leaving, according to local legend, they gave the dies for casting the silver dollars to one of the family members who owned a gristmill in the vicinity. A search of historical records reveals that a nephew of James Yoachum owned and operated the largest gristmill in the Ozarks at the time.

The brothers loaded their wagons and with their families left the Ozarks for California and were never seen in the area again. While their fate may never be known, for many years it was told around the James River Valley that the brothers, along with their families, died crossing the Rocky Mountains on their way to California. With their death went knowledge of the secret location of the silver mine in the Ozarks.

Jacob Levi Yoachum, the son of James, related a story to his son, Tom, that his father told him following the last visit from the federal agents. He said that after the agents departed, all three of the brothers went to the cave and sealed it so no one could ever find it. Jacob often heard James describe the country in the area of the silver mine. He searched for it on several occasions but was never able to find it. He passed his knowledge on to his son, Tom, who lived for many years in Galena, Missouri. Though Tom made several forays deep into the Ozarks, he was never able to find the silver mine either.

The tale of the Yoachum silver dollars and the lost silver mine has been told and retold many times during the past century and a half. As with most legends, each telling has embellished the story. There are, in fact, several versions related to how the brothers originally discovered the mine. In addition to the one presented here, another claims the Yoachum brothers clandestinely watched Indians carrying silver out of the cave. The brothers allegedly killed the Indians, concealed the entrance of the cave against discovery by others, and altered the trail so that it no longer led to the cave.

Another version claims that the brothers had no silver mine at all and that the silver used in the manufacture of the coins was simply recast federal-issued coin. Before the arrival of the Yoachum brothers in the James River Valley, the federal government program of relocating Indians was already in place. In addition to assigning lands to the Indians, each family was provided an annuity of four thousand dollars in silver currency. The Yoachums, greedy for the silver, according to this legend, began making and selling liquor to the Delaware. Not wishing to be caught with Indian money, the Yoachums melted the coins down and recast the silver using their own homemade dies. To cover their illegal activities, the brothers claimed the silver came from a secret Spanish mine they discovered back in the mountains. The reason the Yoachums were so reluctant to reveal the location of the mine to the federal agents and others was, according to this story, because the mine never existed.

This version suggests that the Yoachum brothers possessed certain outlaw tendencies. Some documents found at the Missouri Historical Society tend to confirm this. A man named Joseph Campbell, who was at one time the Indian agent for the James River region, had the responsibility of reporting on unscrupulous white settlers who were taking advantage of the Delawares. In 1822, Campbell prepared a list of such suspects and it included the names James and Solomon Yoachum, both of them involved with selling liquor to the Indians. The third brother was run out of the region for not paying a filing fee on his land.

Yet another story has the Yoachum brothers resettling just outside the border of the Indian lands near the mouth of the Finley River, where they set up whiskey and brandy stills. An attached note stated that the Yoachums manufactured the finest peach brandy in the area.

According to a researcher named Lynn Morrow, the Yoachums knew that their silver coin scheme was to be short-lived. When the Delaware Indians were moved out of the Ozark Mountains and relocated in Indian Territory as a result of the James Fork Treaty of 1829, the Yoachum's source of silver left with them. Morrow noted that after the Indians left, the Yoachum dollars became scarce.

Whichever version of the legend one chooses to accept, the truth remains that the Yoachum dollars did exist and that thousands of them were in circulation at the time.

A man named Homer Johnson, a longtime resident of the southwestern Missouri Ozarks near Bread Tray Mountain, related a story that concerned his grandfather, Jefferson Johnson. Jefferson's boyhood friend was Robert Yoachum, a son of Jacob Levi Yoachum, and as children the two often played together. One afternoon as the two boys were saddling horses in the Yoachum barn, Jefferson spied a barrel nearly filled to the top with Yoachum silver dollars. He estimated there were several thousand of them. What became of that barrel full of Yoachum dollars remains a mystery to this day.

A number of the Yoachum dollars have been found and are in the hands of collectors. Thousands more remain to be discovered. In 1974, a St. Louis man reported that while he was metal detecting near Branson, Missouri, he encountered a cache of 236 large silver coins. He described them as being two inches in diameter and each bearing the inscription "Yoachum" on one side.

Researchers have long wondered what became of the original dies used in casting the Yoachum dollars. They were presumed lost until a remarkable discovery was made on March 11, 1983. A man named J. R. Bunk of Galena was digging near a riverbank on some property not far from the site of the original Yoachum settlement on the James River. Bunk unearthed a large mass of wax. He broke open the ball of wax and inside found two short sections of iron rod. Scraping the wax from the end of one of the rods, Bunk spotted the reverse lettering of the name "Yoachum." On the other rod he found the reverse of "1 Dollar."

Thrilled by this discovery, Bunk spent the next several months researching the Yoachum silver dollar legend and mystery. In the process, he encountered the names of several collectors who owned some of the original coins. Through one of the collectors, Bunk obtained a Yoachum dollar and, on close examination, discovered that it had been stamped by one of the dies he had found. The dies were further examined by a professional numismatist named Fred Wineberg, who opined that the Yoachum coins were formed with the dies in Bunk's possession.

The mystery remains. What happened to the thousands of other Yoachum dollars that were stored in a barrel in the old Yoachum barn?

How many of the coins in circulation were hidden or cached when the federal government forbade their circulation? How many of the Yoachum dollars lie in some old trunk stored in a dusty attic?

And what of the mine shaft in which the original silver mine existed? Did the Yoachums conceal it so well that it can never be found, as was their plan?

Most treasure hunters don't believe the shaft was completely hidden such that it could not be found unless it was covered by a landslide. The evidence suggests that the mine exists, and the tendency of most who have studied this amazing Ozark tale is to believe that a significant number of Spanish smelted silver ingots still lie within, waiting to be rediscovered.

15

THE BEALE TREASURE

One of the most famous lost treasures in America is the so-called Beale Treasure. This compelling tale of a mysterious and elusive cache of what may amount to three thousand pounds of gold, over five thousand pounds of silver, and thirteen thousand dollars' worth of jewels in early-nineteenth-century values has fascinated and tempted treasure hunters for two hundred years. Over time, this treasure has been the subject of books, magazine articles, and television programs. A network news broadcast once stated that the search for the Beale Treasure was one of the longest and costliest in the history of the United States.

In spite of the fact that this treasure has never been found, there exist specific directions to the cache. They are manifested in three separate codes that were devised by the man himself, Thomas Jefferson Beale. One of the codes has been deciphered. The other two, each more complex than the first, have been examined for decades by cryptoanalysts and by computer and decoding experts. They remain unbroken. As a result, the location of this amazing treasure has baffled experts for generations and remains as much of a mystery today as it was when it was buried by Beale in Bedford County, Virginia, in 1819 and 1821.

Little is known of Beale or where he came from. What is known is that early in the year 1817, he and twenty-nine other Virginians traveled westward into New Mexico and Colorado. There are two conflicting stories regarding Beale's reason for leaving Virginia. One has him shooting a neighbor in the town of Fincastle during a fight over a woman. Believing the man dead and fearing that he would be hung for the deed if caught, Beale fled west. The other story has Beale organizing a group of friends to go on a buffalo-hunting and fur-trapping expedition to the western plains and mountains. Neither of these explanations has been verified.

Regardless of what motivated Beale to head west, he and his companions eventually found themselves in south-central Colorado searching for a pass into the higher reaches of the Rocky Mountains where they hoped to find abundant beaver to trap. As the party climbed the foothills of the great range, one of the men discovered a thick vein of gold ore in some exposed rock. They decided on the spot that mining the gold would provide more profit than trapping and selling furs. A few of the men had mining experience, and over the next year and a half they systematically excavated the precious metal from the granite rock matrix of the mountainside. Within a few weeks and a short distance away, they also encountered a vein of silver. Large quantities of both ores were mined.

After eighteen months, the men had accumulated an impressive stockpile of gold and silver. All good friends, they agreed to split the fortune evenly and decided to send Beale, along with eight others, back to Virginia to bury the hoard in a safe place. The others would keep digging the ore from the mountain while awaiting the return of the nine men.

On one bitterly cold afternoon in late November, Beale and his eight companions, along with two wagonloads of gold and silver nuggets, arrived at Goose Creek in Bedford County, Virginia. They followed a narrow and seldom-used trail that paralleled the creek and led into a gap in the foothills of the Blue Ridge Mountains near the Peak of the Otters. Once in the pass, Beale searched around until he found what he wanted—a suitable place to bury the treasure.

As the men worked at excavating a square pit six feet deep, snow began to fall and the wind picked up. As the storm swirled around them, the miners lined the walls and the floor of the pit with flat stones they found nearby. Into this crude earthen vault they placed the gold and silver from all of the months of hard work in the Colorado mines. The gold and silver nuggets were packed into iron cooking pots, the covers tightly secured with wire. The men then filled the hole to the top and covered it over with rocks and forest debris.

Their task accomplished, Beale and his party rested for several days before undertaking the journey back to Colorado. They purchased supplies and fresh horses and departed during the first week of December. They made good time and rejoined their fellow miners at the end of winter.

The mining of the gold and silver ore continued, and after two more years another shipment was readied for the trip back to Virginia to be buried with the earlier cache. Beale was once again selected to lead the expedition. All of the men agreed to keep mining the ore until they had enough gold and silver for a third and final trip to Virginia. On arriving with the last wagonload of ore, they intended to unearth the rich cache, divide the ore, and return to their normal lives as wealthy men.

During a morning in the third week of November 1821, the wagons were loaded to capacity and readied for the second long trip. Bidding farewell to the men who remained to dig more ore, Beale and his friends set out for the Blue Ridge Mountains.

After arriving at the cache site, Beale and his companions added the second load of gold and silver. When the hole was refilled and camouflaged, the men decided to write a description of the secret location and its contents and leave it in the area for the others to find should something happen to them. During the next several days, Beale and his friends devised a series of complex codes. They filled three sheets of paper, each page covered with a series of numerals. These three papers have since been given the name "The Beale Code." They have mystified researchers for almost two centuries.

Cipher Number One allegedly tells how to find the treasure cache. It remains unbroken to this day. Cipher Number Two describes the complete contents of the treasure vault. Cipher Number Three allegedly lists the names of the thirty men who were to divide the treasure.

When the ciphers were completed they were placed in a metal strongbox that was fastened with a stout lock. By agreement, the nine men who developed the code gave the box to an acquaintance named Robert Morris. Morris was a quiet man, often described as a gentleman, who operated a respectable inn at the city of Lynchburg. He often kept valuables for travelers. He was well known to all of the miners and it was agreed he could be trusted to assume charge of the strongbox.

At Morris's invitation, the miners stayed at his inn for several days. When they left for Colorado, Beale told Morris that if someone did not return for the strongbox and its contents, that he, Morris, was to open it. Beale told Morris that within a few weeks he would mail him the information he would need to decode and interpret the information he found in the box. A few days later, Beale and his companions bade Morris good-bye and rode away. Morris watched them disappear down the trail and into the dense forest to the west. He never saw them again.

Two months later, Morris received a short letter from Beale that had been mailed from St. Louis. The letter reiterated what Beale already told Morris—that the contents of the strongbox would be meaningless without the decoding keys. He said the necessary keys were in a sealed envelope with Morris's address on it. The envelope, according to Beale, had been given to a friend in St. Louis with instructions to mail it to Morris in June 1832. Morris never again heard from Beale, nor did he receive the envelope ten years later.

Although the designated time had elapsed, the honorable Morris refused to open the strongbox, thinking that Beale or someone from his party would eventually return to claim it. More time passed, and Morris forgot about the strongbox that had been hidden away under some clutter in an old shed behind the inn. One day, about twenty-three years later, Morris was searching through the shed for a harness when he spotted it.

After some difficulty, Morris broke open the lock and opened the strongbox. The first thing he saw was a letter addressed to him lying atop the other contents. In elaborate detail, the letter described the expeditions of Beale and his companions to the west, the discovery of gold and silver, and the subsequent trips back to the Blue Ridge Mountains to bury the treasure. The letter ended by asking Morris to use the code to locate and dig up the treasure. Morris was to divide it into thirty-one equal portions—one for each of the miners and one for himself.

Morris examined the three pages of ciphers that were in the box, the Beale Code. Each contained what appeared to be a random series of numbers, ranging from single to quadruple digits. Intrigued, Morris spent many hours trying to decipher the curious arrangements of numbers, but in the end could not make any sense of them. Off and on for the next several years, Morris tried to decipher the complex Beale Code, but he eventually gave up.

A few more years passed, and when Morris was convinced no one from Beale's party was going to return to claim the strongbox and its contents, he showed the letters and codes to a friend, James Ward. For months, Ward pored over the three pages and eventually broke Cipher Number Two. Purely by accident, Ward discovered the code was based on the Declaration of Independence. After several days of intensive effort, Ward had the message written out in its entirety. It read:

> I have deposited in the county of Bedford about four miles from Buford's Inn in an excavation or vault six feet below the surface of the ground the following articles belonging to the parties whose names are given in number three herewith. The first deposit was ten hundred and fourteen pounds of gold and thirty-eight hundred pounds of silver. This was deposited November, 1819. The second deposit was made December, 1821, and consisted of nineteen hundred and seven pounds of gold and twelve hundred and eighty-eight pounds of silver. Also jewels obtained in St. Louis in exchange to save transportation and valued at thirteen thousand dollars. The above is packed securely in iron pots with iron covers. The vault is lined with stones and the vessels lie on solid rock with other stones. Paper number one describes the exact location of the vault so no difficulty will be had in finding it.

Ward, suspecting the other two pages would likewise be deciphered by using the Declaration of Independence, eagerly tackled them. He was soon disappointed to learn that their interpretations were based on something else entirely.

Ward was particularly interested in breaking Cipher Number One, the one that allegedly provided directions to the location of the treasure cache, but could make no sense of it whatsoever. Over the years, hundreds have attempted to break the code, but none have succeeded. Below is the code in its entirety:

Beale Cipher Number One
71, 194, 38, 1701, 89, 76, 11, 83, 1629, 48, 94, 63, 132, 16, 111, 95, 84, 341
975, 14, 40, 64, 27, 81, 139, 213, 63, 90, 1120, 8, 15, 3, 126, 2018, 40, 74,
758, 485, 604, 230, 436, 664, 582, 150, 251, 284, 308, 231, 124, 211, 486,
225, 401, 370, 11 101, 305, 139, 189, 17, 33, 88, 208, 193, 145, 1, 94, 73,

416, 918, 263, 28, 500, 538, 356, 117, 136, 219, 27, 176, 130, 10, 460, 25,
485, 18, 436, 65, 84, 200, 283, 118, 320, 138, 36, 416, 280, 15, 71, 224, 961,
44, 16, 401, 39, 88, 61, 304, 12, 21, 24, 283, 134, 92, 63, 246, 486, 682, 7,
219, 184, 360, 780, 18, 64, 463, 474, 131, 160, 79, 73, 440, 95, 18, 64, 581,
34, 69, 128, 367, 461, 17, 81, 12, 103, 820, 62, 116, 97, 103, 862, 70, 60,
1317, 471, 540, 208, 121, 890, 346, 36, 150, 59, 568, 614, 13, 120, 63, 219,
812, 2160, 1780, 99, 35, 18, 21, 126, 872, 15, 28, 170, 88, 4, 30, 44, 112, 18,
147, 436, 195, 320, 37, 122, 113, 6, 140, 8, 120, 305, 42, 58, 461, 44, 106,
301, 13, 408, 680, 93, 86, 116, 530, 82, 568, 9, 10238, 416, 89, 71, 216, 728,
965, 818, 2, 38, 121, 195, 14, 326, 148, 234, 18, 55, 131, 234, 361, 824, 5,
81, 623, 48, 961, 19, 26, 33, 10, 1101, 365, 92, 88, 181, 275, 346, 201, 206,
86, 36, 219, 320, 829, 840, 68, 326, 19, 48, 122, 65, 216, 284, 919, 861, 326,
985, 233, 64, 68, 232, 431, 960, 50, 29, 81, 216, 321, 703, 14, 612, 81, 360,
36, 51, 62, 194, 78, 60, 200, 314, 676, 112, 4, 28, 18, 61, 136, 247, 819, 921,
1060, 464, 895, 10, 6, 66, 119, 38, 41, 49, 612, 423, 962, 302, 294, 875, 78,
14, 23, 111, 109, 62, 31, 501, 823, 216, 280, 34, 24, 150, 1000, 162, 286, 19,
21, 17, 340, 19, 242, 31, 86, 234, 140, 607, 115, 33, 191, 67, 104, 86, 52, 88,
16, 80, 121, 67, 95, 122, 216, 548, 96, 11, 201, 77, 364, 218, 65, 667, 890,
236, 154, 211, 10, 98, 34, 119, 56, 216, 119, 71, 218, 1164, 1496, 1817, 51,
39, 210, 36, 3, 19, 540, 232, 22, 141, 617, 84, 290, 80, 46, 207, 411, 150, 29,
38, 46, 172, 85, 194, 36, 261, 543, 897, 624, 18, 212, 416, 127, 931, 19, 4,
63, 96, 12, 101, 418, 16, 140, 230, 460, 538, 19, 27, 88, 612, 1431, 90, 716,
275, 74, 83, 11, 426, 89, 72, 84, 1300, 1706, 814, 221, 132, 40, 102, 34, 858,
975, 1101, 84, 16, 79, 23,, 16, 81, 122, 324, 403, 912, 227, 936, 447, 55, 86,
34, 43, 212, 108, 96, 314, 264, 1065, 323, 428, 601, 203, 124, 95, 216, 814,
2906, 654, 820, 2, 301, 112, 176, 213, 71, 87, 96, 202, 35, 10, 2, 41, 17, 84,
221, 736, 820, 214, 11, 60, 760.

Ward worked on the two unbroken codes for months before deciding he was getting nowhere. In frustration, he gave up. With permission from Morris, Ward made the codes public. Since then hundreds of people—cryptographers, computer programmers, historians, treasure hunters, adventurers, mystics, and others—have attempted to decipher them, with no success. The Blue Ridge Mountains in and around Bedford County saw visits from thousands who arrived, each believing he would be the one to find the treasure. To date, it is still hidden in the treasure vault where Beale and his companions placed it almost two centuries ago.

The Beale Treasure is considered the best known in Virginia. Some regard it as one of the richest and most elusive lost treasures in America. It is also one of the most sought after. In spite of this, there are some who contend that it is nothing more than an elaborate hoax, and that the treasure never existed. In fact, there are a few who claim that the man Thomas Jefferson Beale never existed. A handful of skeptics have suggested that innkeeper Robert Morris and his friend James Ward fabricated the entire story. As evidence, they point out that Thomas Jefferson, the third President of the United States and author of the Declaration of Independence, on which one cipher was based, had a penchant for writing in numerical codes and ciphers. It is also worth noting that a man named Beale brought word to the east of the gold discoveries in California during the early 1800s.

If the Beale Treasure is a hoax, there are two important questions that must be answered. First, what would have been the purpose of such a deception? On analysis, there appears to have been no obvious or profitable motive for such a sophisticated and elaborate trick. Neither Morris nor Ward ever profited from their association with the Beale Treasure, and both reportedly shunned any kind of publicity whatsoever. Second, the sheer intricacy of the codes makes it unlikely that they were devised merely as a prank.

In the final analysis, most researchers are convinced that the Beale Treasure does exist and in the exact amounts described by T. J. Beale himself in Cipher Number Two.

16

INCAN TREASURE IN TEXAS
AND AMERICA'S FIRST BIBLE

Professional treasure hunters agree that one of the most amazing and puzzling tales of buried treasure in the country involves a lost Inca cache of unimaginable wealth buried somewhere near the Salt Fork of the Brazos River on the Texas High Plains. This treasure, believed by researchers to be worth more than two hundred million dollars, consists of forty mule loads of gold and silver ingots, emeralds described to be "as large as goose eggs," and hundreds of jewels consisting of precious stones arranged in artistically crafted settings of pure gold and silver. What may be even more valuable, at least to historians, is the probability that the cache contains what is believed by many to be the first copy of the Holy Bible to arrive in the New World.

❖

In 1531, the ruthless and bloodthirsty Spanish explorer Francisco Pizarro led a force of nearly two hundred armed and mounted soldiers into the remote regions of Peru, South America. Accompanying the soldiers was the normal contingent of cooks, herders, livestock, priests, and women. Among the possessions of one of the priests was the first Bible carried to the New World. The Spaniards, in their lust for conquest and riches, attacked and looted every village they encountered, killing men, women, and children. They seized whatever wealth they could find in the form of gold, silver, precious stones, and jewels. Before long, their pack animals staggered under the weight of the wealth they transported across the mountains and through the valleys.

After many weeks, the Spaniards arrived at the large Incan village of Cotapampas in the Andean foothills. Here they found even larger quantities of gold, silver, and other riches. With little hesitation, they attacked and seized the city, killing dozens of citizens in the process. When questioning several elders as to the source of the gold and other wealth, Pizarro was informed of the city of Cajamarca, located six hundred miles to the northwest. Cajamarca, it was explained, was a veritable storehouse of gold, silver, and emeralds. Eager to locate this great city of riches, Pizarro enslaved several of the Cotapampas Indians and forced them to guide his soldiers to Cajamarca.

Around the middle of November 1532, Pizarro and his army arrived at the outskirts of Cajamarca, a city of two thousand residents. Pizarro sent one of his priests, along with one of the Cotapampans to serve as a translator, to seek an audience with the region's ruler, Atahualpa.

When Atahualpa appeared, he was informed by the priest that he and his people must immediately accept the teachings of Christianity, deliver all weapons to the gate, and allow the Spaniards to take possession of the city. The priest then pressed a Bible into Atahualpa's hands. Surprised, and then angered, at the demands of the strangers, Atahualpa threw the Bible to the ground and ordered the gates of the city closed to the newcomers.

The Spaniards, seasoned warriors all, wasted little time in attacking the city. Crashing through the gate, they swarmed through Cajamarca, indiscriminately clubbing, slashing, and spearing anything that moved. Though vastly outnumbered, the Spaniards were better armed and trained in warfare than the Indians. Two hours later the few hundred Cajamarcan survivors, including Atahualpa, were taken prisoner. During the ensuing week, even these poor souls were subjected to horrible torture and ultimately death.

At the end of the week, Atahualpa was among the handful of survivors. Chained at the wrists and ankles, he, along with a dozen Indians, was brought before Pizarro and made to kneel. Pizarro then ordered the remaining Indians to travel to the outlying villages and inform the leaders that if they did not bring in all of their gold, silver, and precious stones, that Atahualpa would be slain. For the next several weeks the runners reached every village within one hundred miles of Cajamarca and soon the wealth was being delivered. By the time six weeks had passed, three entire rooms were filled to the ceiling with gold and silver ore, ornaments, jewelry, and statuary, along with heavy packs of emeralds.

While at Cajamarca, Pizarro learned of a city far to the north called Quito, a location believed to have a huge storehouse of gold, silver, and stones. He quickly ordered a contingent of soldiers, along with a priest and translator, to travel to that city, seize the wealth, and return with it to Cajamarca. When the party of Spaniards arrived at Quito, however, the citizens there mounted a resistance, and fighting broke out that lasted several days.

When Quito's treasure had not arrived within the appointed time, Pizarro ordered a dozen soldiers under the command of a trusted captain to travel to the area to look into the delay. When the soldiers arrived several days later, they joined in the fighting and in a short time the city was taken. The captain soon discovered that, indeed, the treasure of this northern city was quite impressive. He immediately commandeered a number of llamas to transport the gold, silver, and jewels.

As the captain watched the treasure being packed, he marveled at the vast fortune that passed before his eyes: thousands of bars of gold as well as huge emeralds set in magnificent gold and silver necklaces, rings, and earrings. The more the captain considered this incredible fortune, the more he thought about the possibilities of keeping it for himself. Finally, convinced he could be wealthy beyond his wildest dreams, he devised a plan wherein he, along with some trusted companions, would escape to the north with the largest portion of the treasure.

Along with six soldiers who were not part of his scheme, the captain sent several llama loads of treasure back to Cajamarca, explaining that the rest of the contingent would depart the following day and meet them at the city. By the time the first pack train was well down the trail, however, the captain and his followers, along with a number of Indians who were taken as slaves, herded the second and larger pack train toward the north.

Accompanying the captain was the priest, who traveled on foot carrying only a small pack containing his belongings. Among these was the Bible offered to Atahualpa.

As the small party led the treasure-laden llamas northward along the ridges of the Andean mountains, far to the south Pizarro, despite his promises to the contrary, had Atahualpa slain. The three rooms of treasure that had been accumulated were loaded onto every available pack animal. This done, Pizarro led his bloodthirsty soldiers on a killing and looting rampage across much of what is now Ecuador, Colombia, and Peru, taking gold, silver, and jewels and adding to the already immense load of riches they had accumulated. Pizarro's zest for conquest, along with his numerous successes, distracted him from the issue of the desertion of his trusted captain and the loss of a portion of the Quito treasure. As a result, he never got around to organizing pursuit and, in time, simply forgot about the matter altogether.

For many months the traitorous captain and his followers led the treasure-laden llamas northward across the high mountain reaches, dense jungles, and arid deserts. They passed out of the mountains and traveled the narrow Isthmus of Panama, up through the steamy jungles of Central America and southern Mexico, and in time crossed the Rio Grande into present-day Texas.

During this time several of the Indians and two of the Spaniards were lost to fever, two of the slaves had been whipped to death, and the remainder of the party often suffered from hunger and thirst. Though their clothes had been reduced to little more than dirty rags and their boots had long since worn out, the captain kept the soldiers encouraged by telling them of his dreams of establishing a new kingdom at a location some place farther north, one financed by the riches they transported, one in which they would all be wealthy men. When, after a time, his vision of a regime failed to inspire them, he would warn them that Pizarro had likely sent a contingent of soldiers in pursuit. With thoughts of the horrible tortures that would be inflicted on them should they be captured, the Spaniards found new strength and continued their northward march.

Throughout the hardships faced by the travelers, the captain managed to keep precise notes of their progress on a piece of tanned leather. Included with the notes was a detailed map. One afternoon as the party was setting up camp near a pair of low mountains, the captain made meticulous additions to his leather journal and included sketches of all of the nearby landmarks. Many years later it was discerned as a result of interpreting this map that the site of the camp was near the Double Mountains in Stonewall County, Texas, between the Salt Fork of the

Brazos River and the present-day town of Aspermont in the Texas Panhandle.

As the captain carefully worked on this map, one of his soldiers approached and informed him that they were being watched by Indians. Looking up from his work, the captain spotted several dozen armed warriors observing the Spaniards from a nearby ridge.

There was little sleep for the group that night, and it was a nervous party that broke camp the following morning and continued on their journey. As they traveled, they noted they were followed by the Indians and that their numbers had increased.

After passing Double Mountains on their northward trek, the Spaniards halted at the south bank of the Salt Fork. Convinced that the Indians were preparing to attack, the captain made a decision: they would unload the treasure from the llamas, bury it at this location, and then flee unencumbered. When they were certain the threat of attack was over they would return, retrieve the treasure, and continue on their journey and with their dreams of a kingdom.

During a time when they were not being observed by the Indians, the captain ordered the slaves to excavate twenty-one holes, each of them six to eight feet deep. The treasure from the pack animals was divided and placed into the holes. As the holes were being refilled, the priest, after wrapping the Bible tightly in a piece of soft leather, placed it in one of the excavations atop the treasure. Once the holes were refilled, the pack animals were led back and forth across them, completely obliterating any sign of digging. That evening, the Spaniards set up camp and constructed a rude fortification in case they were forced to defend themselves against an Indian attack. The captain made more entries on his piece of leather, detailing the location of the buried Incan treasure.

With the threat of attack diminished for the time being, the captain decided to remain at the location for several more days. Once he was certain the Indians no longer posed a threat, he would have the treasure dug up and they would continue on their journey.

At this point, the tale grows murky, and it was never determined what became of the Spaniards. The record of their journey, as manifested on the piece of leather, ends at this point. Some researchers suggest that the group continued northward and eventually succumbed to thirst and starvation. Others maintain that they were eventually victims of the Indian attack they feared. Evidence for the latter was discovered in 1887 in the form of numerous skeletons—human and llama—along with Spanish armor and weaponry near Kiowa Peak in the northeastern part of Stonewall County. The all-important leather document maintained by the Spanish captain was not found there, but it appeared many years later.

Following the Civil War, the American West, and especially Texas, opened up to settlers fleeing the war-torn South. The Panhandle region of Texas along with its lush prairie grasses appealed to many, and in a short time small farming and ranching settlements sprang up across the High Plains. Even during that time, a tale of long-lost Incan treasure buried somewhere in the Panhandle was passed among residents and newcomers. No organized attempt, however, was ever undertaken to try to locate and retrieve it.

A noteworthy event occurred in 1876. An elderly Spaniard driving an expensive black lacquered carriage pulled by two blooded horses arrived in Stonewall County and immediately began purchasing parcels of land near the Double Mountain region of the Salt Fork. The Spaniard spoke to very few people, preferring to conduct his business quietly and confidentially. Most of the county's residents presumed the newcomer was interested in establishing a ranch, but it soon became clear that was not his intention.

The Spaniard erected a tent at a certain location on his property. Then, as suddenly as he appeared, he vanished, riding away in his carriage late one night, never to return. After he left, several local residents rode out to his holdings to have a look around. What they discovered was indeed strange. Here and there at one location they found buckets and shovels and other tools lying about as if suddenly abandoned. Even more curious, they discovered a total of ten holes, each one six to eight feet deep. It was clear from the markings found inside the holes that they once contained packs and crates.

Those familiar with the tale of the buried Inca treasure in the area were convinced the Spaniard found some of it and carried it away. How the stranger managed to transport such a sizeable amount of the heavy gold, silver, and other treasures was never determined. No one ever discovered his identity or where he went. What was quickly discerned, however, was that there remained eleven holes unexcavated.

During the ensuing years, floods from the Salt Fork have filled the ten excavations with sediment. While there were some old-timers in the county who claimed to know where these holes could be found, there exists some confusion about the actual location of the ten excavated holes.

Strange, indeed, but events were about to get even stranger.

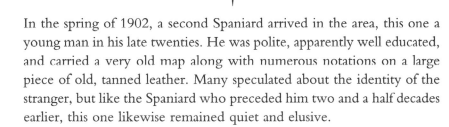

In the spring of 1902, a second Spaniard arrived in the area, this one a young man in his late twenties. He was polite, apparently well educated, and carried a very old map along with numerous notations on a large piece of old, tanned leather. Many speculated about the identity of the stranger, but like the Spaniard who preceded him two and a half decades earlier, this one likewise remained quiet and elusive.

After spending several days riding around the property purchased by the earlier Spaniard, the younger one rode into Aspermont, purchased a number of shovels, picks, and buckets, and hired four men to do some digging. One of the men, who was interviewed several years later, stated that the young Spaniard, constantly consulting the leather map, led the diggers around the area for four days checking landmarks and asking questions about the region. Finally, they arrived at a location decided upon by the young man and commenced digging.

Within the first hour of labor, the workers unearthed four skeletons. They were then directed to excavate other holes at marked locations. Several of these holes appeared to have been previously excavated and then filled in with river sediment. Though the workers dug as deep as eight feet into the ground, nothing was found.

On the day they were due to be paid, the Spaniard explained that he did not have enough money but that he would share a percentage of the treasure he claimed they were certain to find. Following several more days of digging in the hot Panhandle sun and finding nothing, the workers grew irritable and demanded their wages. The Spaniard told them he would go into town and obtain some money from the bank. After carefully folding the leather map and placing it into a case, he climbed aboard his carriage and drove away. It was the last anyone ever saw of him.

Most researchers who have studied this tale are convinced that the young Spaniard was related to the one who had arrived years earlier, perhaps a son or a grandson. They are also convinced that the reason he did not find any of the buried Incan treasure is that the workers dug into the same holes previously excavated by the elderly Spaniard years earlier.

As far as anyone knows, the remaining eleven caches have never been found and remain filled with a great portion of the Incan treasure. In one of them lies, many contend, the first Bible to reach the Americas.

17

LOST TREASURE IN THE MONAHANS SANDHILLS

Located near the point where Winkler, Ector, Crane, and Ward counties all come together in West Texas near the northern limit of Big Bend country, an expanse of bright sand dunes rises out of the otherwise gravelly and creosote-studded desert floor. From an airplane, this unbroken collection of dunes looks much like an island, and there is no place else like it in Texas.

So unique and spectacular are these sands that they have been designated by Texas as Monahans Sandhills State Park, a travel destination that receives thousands of visitors each year. Unknown to those who come, however, and lying somewhere just inches below the very dunes they hike and play on, are the remains of forty wagons along with 477 gold ingots. This lost treasure is estimated to be worth in excess of thirty-five million dollars today.

$$\clubsuit$$

In Yuma, Arizona, in September 1873, preparations were being made for the departure of a wagon train on a long journey to St. Louis, Missouri. The party of travelers consisted of several dozen families of Dutch descent. Years earlier, they had traveled to California to seek their fortunes in the gold fields. By dint of frugal living, hard work, and a modicum of luck at locating and harvesting gold ore, they grew wealthy. The gold-laced quartz outcrops in the California Rockies yielded the mineral they came for. They mined, panned, smelted, and stored the gold until they were convinced they had accumulated enough to establish a Dutch settlement at a preselected location along the Missouri–Illinois border.

With their newfound wealth, the leaders of the Dutch party purchased the finest wagons, horses, and oxen for the long trip. Along with supplies, rifles, and ammunition, the gold was loaded onto several of the wagons and covered with the possessions of the families. It was early autumn, and the travelers were anxious to begin the trek eastward before the weather turned cold.

During the first several weeks travel was difficult. The party endured storms, floods, drought, and Indian attacks. A few attempts were made by outlaws to rob the wagon train but they were repelled by the Dutch marksmen. Three months from the time they began their journey in Yuma, they reached Horsehead Crossing on the Pecos River in West Texas. Minutes after the last wagon made it across the river, the leader of the Dutch party, a man named Daniel Flake, spotted several mounted Indians watching the caravan from a nearby rise. Flake rode toward the Indians to apologize for the intrusion into their territory and to inform them they were only passing through.

As Flake approached the Indians he noted that they were armed with bows, arrows, and lances. Their faces and bodies were painted. When he was fifty yards from their position, the Indians turned their horses and galloped away down an adjacent ravine. Flake had come close enough to the Indians to recognize them as Comanches. He also knew they were one of the most feared tribes in North America and one known to attack and slay travelers who entered their realm. That night, Flake ordered the guard doubled around the wagon train.

For the next few days as the wagon train lumbered eastward, Flake observed Comanches watching them from a distance. When he and other riders attempted to approach, the Indians rode away, disappearing into the landscape. Flake grew nervous with the Indians' presence, and confessed to a bad feeling. He told one of the stock handlers that he was having premonitions of disaster.

Travel was slow, the tired oxen managing only a few miles each day. More time passed, and one day the wagon train rolled through the tiny settlement of Monahans, a community that consisted of little more than ragged tents and brush shelters. On reaching the eastern outskirts of Monahans, a scout rode up to Flake and informed him of a large expanse of sand dunes a short distance ahead. Within its limit, the scout said, he found a freshwater spring and suggested it would be a good place to camp for the night. Flake led the party toward the dunes.

As the wagon train approached the destination, Flake again noticed they were being watched by Comanches. The Indians were on horseback and remained two hundred yards behind them. Flake counted more than one hundred and fifty warriors. He also noted that each was carrying a weapon.

Around midday, the wagon train entered the dunes. The mounds of shiny, light-colored sand grains extended east and north as far as Flake could see. Many of the dunes were dozens of feet tall. The varying topography, along with the soft sand, made travel difficult for the oxen and horses. Moving through the yielding ground and sinking several inches into the sand was much more difficult than walking across the hard-packed desert floor they had experienced up until now. Before much time had passed, the animals had become exhausted.

The wheels of the heavy wagons sank even deeper into the sands, sometimes causing forward movement to cease altogether and necessitating the efforts of men and additional draft animals to pull the vehicles free. As the Dutch fought the challenges of these obstacles while making their way to the freshwater spring, the Comanches were making their way closer to the wagon train. While hitching extra oxen to a wagon that had sunk into deep sand, Flake looked up and spotted the Indians sitting their ponies only fifty yards away.

It was well past sundown by the time the party reached the spring. Flake ordered the drivers to pull the wagons into a protective circle in the event the Indians decided to launch a strike. This done, he instructed the women and children to fill the water barrels from the nearby spring.

That night, the waxing moon shone bright in the sky. Flake and several of the men stood guard around the wagons. In the distance, they could see the Comanche warriors riding their mounts slowly back and forth, deliberately circling the campsite. Throughout the night, the Indians rode in an ever-widening circle. By dawn they were gone.

During the night, a group of men approached Flake and expressed their concern that the Indians knew about their gold and wanted to steal it. Despite Flake's objections, the men insisted the gold ingots be removed from the wagons that night and buried at some location in the dunes. In the morning, the train would depart. When the Indians approached the train and saw there was no gold, they insisted, they would simply ride away. At some time in the future when the Indian menace was removed from the region by the U.S. Army, they would return to the location, dig up the gold, and proceed to their new settlement in the east.

Flake objected strenuously to this proposal, explaining that the Comanches cared nothing at all for the gold, that they were just angered at this intrusion into their lands. If anything, said Flake, the Comanches would be more interested in stealing the horses and oxen than any gold they carried.

Despite Flake's arguments, the group of men insisted their plan be followed. Realizing the futility of further objections, Flake stood by while the men unloaded the gold ingots and buried them in several excavations made inside the circle of wagons.

Flake did not sleep that night. The bad feeling he had been experiencing the previous days returned even stronger. He paced about the camp all night, stopping now and then to peer out into the darkness, searching for any sign of the Comanches. When dawn broke and just before any of the sleeping travelers had awakened, Flake spotted a lone Comanche sitting astride a pony atop a dune some fifty yards away. As Flake watched the Indian for several minutes, the camp began to stir as men and women climbed out of the wagons and started campfires to prepare breakfast. Horses and oxen were tended to and children scurried about playing in the cool dawn.

As the Dutchmen moved about with their morning chores, the lone Indian, in a slow and deliberate movement, raised his lance high above his head. Within seconds, he was joined by the rest of the Comanches, all armed with similar lances as well as bows and arrows, war clubs, and a few rifles.

Flake debated whether or not to approach the Indians. Seconds later, however, the relative quiet of the early morning was shattered by a piercing cry. In another moment, the Comanches galloped down the dunes toward the circle of wagons. Their war cries rang through the air and mixed with the screams of the terrified travelers.

As women and children ran for the shelter of the wagons, the Dutchmen scrambled for their rifles. No sooner had they retrieved their weapons than the Comanches were upon them, riding about the camp inside the wagon circle slashing, clubbing, and shooting all they came in contact with. The skirmish lasted for thirty minutes as the Dutchmen valiantly sought to defend their families. Their efforts proved fruitless. All of the members of the wagon train—men, women, and children— were dead.

When the last of the immigrants were scalped, the Comanches turned to the wagons and began looting them. They found and took cooking pots, clothes, bolts of cloth, and other goods deemed important. Unwanted items were tossed to the ground. Some of the warriors cut the harnesses and reins from the stock and began herding the animals away toward the north.

By noon, all of the wagons had been ransacked and set afire. The last of the Indians had ridden away to join the main band. Already, the convection-driven desert winds were stirring the light sand grains on the desert floor, blowing them along and pushing them up against the remains of the wagons and the scattered and mutilated bodies of more than one hundred Dutch. Buzzards that had been circling high in the sky began their slow, patient descent to the ground. They flew in ever-tightening spirals toward the corpses lying on the blood-soaked sand.

The gold ingots, their total weight estimated to be as much as ten thousand pounds, lay just below a covering of sand in several individual caches. They had gone unseen by the Indians. They would remain there for a long time.

Decades passed, and the ever-shifting sands of the Chihuahuan Desert closed in upon and covered the entire remains of the wagon train. Travelers who stopped at the freshwater spring occasionally told of finding what appeared to be an old wooden plank from a wagon or a piece of harness, but none were aware of the massacre that had taken place there during the early part of 1874.

Other than availing themselves of the cool waters of the spring, people passing through the region had little reason to enter the realm of what had come to be called the Monahans Sandhills. The first formal expedition to enter the area was led by Arthur Hayes, a retired U.S. Army colonel and a prominent West Texas judge. Hayes undertook such expeditions from time to time to evaluate the surrounding countryside to assess the possibilities for the grazing of livestock.

The scout for the Hayes expedition was a man named Robert Brown. Brown led the Hayes party into the Monahans Sandhills and selected a location for camp at the freshwater spring, now called Willow Spring. While encamped here, Hayes and other men found several charred pieces of milled lumber. One of the members of the group suggested they might have come from a wagon. On the second day, they found two wagon wheels and several metal fittings partially buried in the sand.

Curious, some of the men began digging, and in a short time unearthed several dozen human skeletons. A number of the skulls appeared to have been caved in such as might happen from the heavy blow from a club. Some of the bones had stone arrowheads embedded in them.

After piecing together the evidence of what likely occurred at Willow Spring, Hayes tried for several years to solve the mystery of the destroyed wagon train and the death of its members. An elderly man, Hayes passed away before learning the truth.

In the wake of Arthur Hayes, other researchers analyzed remains of the wagon train and eventually concluded the site contained what was left of the Dutch party that left Yuma, Arizona, in 1873 and never arrived at its intended destination in Missouri. Originally, the group had departed Pennsylvania years earlier for California to seek their fortune in the gold fields.

Several years later, one of the researchers encountered an old newspaper clipping describing in detail the organization of a party of Dutch miners in Yuma and their plans to travel to a location in the east to establish a religious community. The researcher was startled to read that the party left Yuma with 477 gold ingots.

Excited at the prospect of locating the treasure, the researcher returned to the site near Willow Springs. On arriving, however, he found that it had once again been covered over by the shifting desert sands. He was unable to relocate the exact place he had excavated years earlier.

During the 1940s, a cowhand employed at a nearby cattle ranch rode into the Monahans Sandhills in search of some stray cattle. He followed their tracks to Willow Spring where he found the animals resting in the shade of the few trees that grew there. Since it was late in the day, the cowhand decided to make camp and herd the cattle back to the ranch in the morning. As he scooped out a small pit in the sand in which to make his campfire, his hand struck something solid. After scraping away more of the sand, he removed a large metal bar. Thinking it was a piece of lead used for fashioning bullets, he placed it in one of his saddlebags. He intended to give it to the ranch foreman, who reloaded his own ammunition for his rifle.

The following day when he returned to the ranch with the cattle, the cowhand unsaddled his mount to groom it. He carried the saddlebags into the bunkhouse, removed the ingot, and slid it under his cot, intending to hand it over to the foreman at the first opportunity. He soon forgot about it. Six months later, the ranch hand accepted an offer for a similar job in Kansas. After working his last day at the Monahans ranch, he told his companions good-bye, shook hands all around, and left. The ingot, forgotten, remained under his cot.

It was months later when another of the cowhands came upon the ingot while trying to locate a rattlesnake that had gotten into the bunkhouse. Upon close inspection, the cowhand determined it was gold. He kept his discovery a secret for weeks while he tried to learn more about it. Finally, he informed the foreman of his find and asked him what he knew about it. The cowhand obtained the name of the previous employee who had occupied the cot and an address of a Kansas ranch. He wrote a letter inquiring about the origin of the ingot.

Weeks later, the cowhand received a letter from the Kansas cowboy who briefly described the circumstances relating to the discovery of the gold bar. He also wrote that he had found it near Willow Spring in the sandhills. The cowhand, along with the foreman, traveled the short distance to Willow Spring to try to find more of the ingots but were unsuccessful.

In the years that have passed since researchers made the connection between the massacre of the Dutch travelers in the Monahans Sandhills and the large amount of gold bars the party was transporting, hopeful treasure hunters have arrived at Monahans Sandhills State Park to try to find this treasure cache. Now and then a piece of metal wagon fitting or charred wood was located, convincing searchers they were in the right place.

In 1992, an old man known for his ability to dowse for water and minerals came to the area. He was hired by a rancher to find underground water so that a well could be dug. The ranch was located north of the sandhills. While the dowser was witching for water, he claimed he received what he called a "strong pull of gold" from some distance to the south. After finding water for the rancher, the dowser said he was going to travel into the sandhills and attempt to determine what was causing his dowsing rod to respond to whatever might be located there.

Though hunting for treasure is against the law in Texas state parks, the dowser nevertheless walked about the dunes following the pull of his dowsing rod. It was a hot August day, and the elderly and somewhat overweight dowser trudged up and down several of the high dunes. The soft sand made walking difficult, and he was forced to stop often to rest.

The dowser entered the dunes from the north, and from his tracks it was clear he had covered several miles in his search, zigzagging his way across the sandhills. He was found the next day, dead from an apparent heart attack. Park rangers encountered him lying face down in the sand, his body stretched out, his dowsing rod still clutched in his weathered fingers. The end of the rod pointed directly toward Willow Spring, less than one hundred yards away.

There have been rumors of other visitors to the Monahans Sandhills State Park who have found some of the gold ingots, but none have been verified. Allegedly, all of the discoveries have occurred near Willow Spring.

Though illegal, treasure hunters continue to arrive at the state park to search for the lost gold ingots, each one hopeful he will be the one to find the lost treasure of the Dutch wagon train. To date, however, the large caches of gold buried there have never been found.

18

CHIEF VICTORIO'S GOLD

The rugged environs of the mountain and desert country of West Texas have long lured treasure hunters. Experienced adventurers claim that this region contains more lost mines and buried treasures than any other area in the United States. One of the richest, and most elusive, treasure caches that has attracted the attention of hundreds is associated with Eagle Mountains.

A remote cave exists somewhere deep in the heart of this range, one that was well known to the Apache Indians who frequented the area during the latter part of the nineteenth century. Many believed that the cave was filled with hundreds of gold ingots stolen by the Indians from Mexican pack trains. The gold was allegedly used by the notorious Apache Chief Victorio for the purpose of acquiring rifles and ammunition, but he only removed a small portion. The bulk of this vast treasure, estimated to be worth many millions of dollars, remains hidden in the cave.

During and following the Civil War, more and more Americans from the war-torn South fled their homelands and journeyed westward. Some had heard of the riches to be gleaned in the gold fields of California and traveled there. Others with more modest goals found something they liked about Texas, and settled into the farming and ranching lands of the central and southern parts of the state. Others—trappers, traders, prospectors, miners, and adventurers—continued westward in search of a living. Some succeeded; others succumbed to the rigors of West Texas drought and Indian attacks. Some found their fortune, only to lose it.

In response to the increasing numbers of travelers, stage lines and railroad companies surveyed and opened up new routes to accommodate the growing number of customers. One stage line wound across the plains and deserts from San Antonio to El Paso. Along the way, it stopped at designated stagecoach stations set up for the purpose of supplying fresh horses, making repairs, and providing accommodations and meals for the passengers.

One of the stations was located at Eagle Springs in the foothills on the northern edge of the Eagle Mountains and fifteen miles southwest of Van Horn. One of the regular stagecoach drivers was a young man named Joe Peacock. Though he was only nineteen years of age, Peacock was already a veteran of several shootouts with outlaws as well as raids by Indians. He was a skilled driver and a dependable employee and soon rose to the ranks of favored worker in the eyes of his supervisors. The stagecoach company was in desperate need of men who manifested the qualities and skills of Peacock to negotiate the coaches through that rugged part of West Texas and keep passengers safe from attacks by hostile Indians and bandits.

It was during this time that the Apache Indian chief Victorio took up residence in the nearby Eagle Mountains. Victorio despised all white men, Spaniards, and Mexicans, and vowed to slay every one with whom he came in contact. From time to time, Victorio and his band were seen riding in the region of the Eagle Springs stagecoach station.

One afternoon, Joe Peacock pulled his stagecoach into the yard of the Eagle Springs station. As he was about to step down off of the coach, twenty warriors charged out of the nearby foothills firing rifles, hurling lances, and shooting arrows into passengers and station employees. Within a few minutes, everyone was dead except for Peacock, who was suffering from an arrow wound in his left thigh. The Apaches decided to take him captive.

Peacock was tied across the back of an Indian pony and led away by one of Victorio's warriors. After leaving the stagecoach station, the Apaches traveled southward across the Rio Grande and into the Tres Castillos Mountains in Mexico. The Tres Castillos range had long served as an Apache stronghold, and Victorio often sought refuge there from pursuing soldiers from both the U.S. and Mexican armies. Here the Indians would rest and tend their horses before launching another raid.

As Peacock rode in his uncomfortable position on the horse, he was convinced he was being saved for some form of horrible torture. Peacock remembered stories about the Apaches and of how they would keep a man alive for hours while subjecting him to great pain, and it made him tremble.

Days later when the party arrived at the Tres Castillos hideout, Peacock was pulled from the horse, untied, and turned over to a young woman named Juanita, who treated his wound. The girl Juanita remains controversial. Some researchers insist she was the daughter of Victorio, others say she was a Mexican captive. When Peacock's wound healed, he was assigned chores around the camp: collecting firewood, hauling water from a spring, tending the fires, and helping to cure hides. He was, for all intents and purposes, a slave.

From time to time Peacock was subjected to beatings by some of the women and warriors when he did not work as hard as they thought he should. Years later he told an interviewer that as long as he lived, he harbored hope that he might find a way to escape.

While Peacock was a captive in Victorio's camp, Juanita found ways to spend time with him. Sometimes at night she would sneak out of her wickiup and crawl to where the captive lay sleeping under a tree. One night Victorio caught Juanita and Peacock together. The Apache chief wanted to kill Peacock, but Juanita pleaded for his life to be spared.

While visiting Peacock, Juanita told him that she would wed him. The statement took the prisoner by surprise. Though Peacock appreciated all that Juanita had done for him and was flattered by her attention, he did not love her. Further, he did not want to refuse her, for she was the only person in the camp responsible for keeping him alive.

Peacock told Juanita a made-up story that he had a very ill mother living in Texas and that he was very concerned for her. He explained that once he was certain his mother was well, he would be free to marry. Juanita accepted Peacock's explanation and was content for a while, but soon she resumed her desire to be wed. During her somewhat aggressive courtship of the prisoner, Juanita told Peacock that if he would consent to marry her she would tell him where Chief Victorio hid all of the gold he had stolen from Mexican pack trains. Peacock had seen a few gold ingots in the camp on several occasions and wondered to himself how and why the Apaches came into possession of them. He learned from Juanita that the Indians used them to barter for rifles and ammunition from Mexican and American gunrunners. The prisoner also watched as Apache artisans fashioned bracelets and other items from the soft metal. The ingots seemed to be plentiful, and Peacock wondered how many Victorio had hidden away in some secret location.

Juanita was aware of Peacock's interest in the gold ingots. She told him that hundreds of the bars were hidden in a small cave in the Eagle Mountains not far from the stagecoach station where he had been taken captive. She explained that there was a well-marked trail that led from the cave to the tiny settlement of Indian Hot Springs on the Rio Grande. The Apaches often stopped at these hot springs going to and from raids. Here they would rest their animals and bathe in the warm waters.

Juanita told Peacock that she had visited the cave many times. She was first taken there as a child and watched as warriors loaded ingots onto pack mules. In addition to the ingots, she said, the cave also contained dozens of leather bags filled with gold coins and nuggets. She told Peacock it would take at least fifty burros to transport all of the gold in the cave.

During one of their conversations, Peacock learned from Juanita that a small party of Apaches had left the camp to travel to the cave to retrieve more ingots. Along the way, they encountered a platoon of U.S. Calvary that gave chase. The Indians sought shelter among the rocks and a brief skirmish ensued. Two of the troopers were killed and one of the Indians wounded. The soldiers retreated, and the Apaches continued on to the cave.

When the party of Indians returned to the hideout in the Tres Castillos Mountains and informed Victorio of the incident, the chief grew furious. He was concerned the soldiers would return in great strength and follow the trail to the cave in the Eagle Mountains and take the gold. Wasting no time, Victorio assembled another group of Indians. He told them to ride to the cave and conceal the entrance by stacking rocks in front of the small opening and then generate a small landslide to cover it. Before departing the area, he told his warriors to take care to make the site look much the same as the rest of the mountain.

For days, Peacock asked Juanita to tell him the location of the treasure cave. She was concerned that he was more interested in the gold than he was in her, and she refused. One day after one of her visits, however, she agreed to tell him where it was and gave him directions. She told him he must not go search for it without her.

However, with knowledge of the treasure, Peacock began making plans to escape from the Tres Castillos hideout. At night while he slept, he dreamed about the fortune that awaited him in the secret cave.

Weeks passed, and Peacock bided his time, ever alert for an opportunity to escape. He was watched closely by the Apaches and when he was sent to gather firewood, a guard went with him. Then, early one morning as he rose from his sleeping pallet under the tree, he spotted Victorio riding about the camp and gathering his warriors. Within minutes, most of the Indians were mounted and heading south deeper into Mexico to conduct raids and take horses. As he looked around the encampment, Peacock noted that the remaining Apaches consisted mostly of old men, women, and children.

That evening, Peacock told Juanita that this afforded the best time to leave for Texas. He promised her he would go see his ailing mother and then return for her as soon as he could. Juanita provided Peacock with a stout pony capable of making the long and rugged journey across the desert. She handed him a saddlebag filled with venison jerky and tortillas and a deer bladder that held a supply of water. Taking care not to arouse any of the Indians, Peacock rode out of the camp, down the mountain, and then north toward the safety of Texas.

Using the directions provided by Juanita, Peacock rode directly to Eagle Springs where he made a small camp not far from the stage station. Exhausted from his long ride, he rested for several days before undertaking the search for Chief Victorio's secret cave. On several occasions, he walked and rode along the trail identified by Juanita as the one that led to the cave, but he had difficulty interpreting the landmarks. A number of locations matched her descriptions but many did not. Peacock grew confused.

For weeks Peacock explored and searched the region but found nothing. He began to wonder if the girl had given him partial directions in the hope that he would return to her.

After one month, Peacock had exhausted his food supply. He needed to find employment so that he could purchase more. A few weeks later, he regained his job as stagecoach driver. In his spare time he continued to search for the cave of gold.

Several years passed. Peacock managed to save enough money from his job to purchase a small ranch not far from the Eagle Mountains. When he was not occupied with working cattle and repairing fence, he returned to the Eagle Mountains to continue his quest to find the gold.

In 1880, Texas Ranger Captain George W. Baylor and another named North led a command into the region between the Eagle Mountains and the Rio Grande. Their orders were to look for renegade Apaches and, if encountered, engage them. Their objective was to capture them. Failing that, they were to kill as many as possible.

Days earlier, Baylor received word that Chief Victorio's band of Apaches had been attacked in their Tres Castillos stronghold by the Mexican army led by General Luis Terrazas. Most of the Indians were killed, but a handful escaped and fled north toward the Rio Grande. The Texas Rangers prepared to intercept them before they had an opportunity to prey on travelers and settlers. It was well known throughout the area that Victorio's Apaches often camped in the Eagle Mountains.

After days of waiting to encounter the Indians, Baylor grew restless. Believing he could more effectively surprise the Apaches before they arrived in the Eagle Mountains, he ordered his contingent of Ranger troopers across the river and into Mexico. Riding with Baylor's command was Joe Peacock. The former stagecoach driver had signed on with the Rangers only two weeks earlier.

Days later, the Rangers arrived in the Tres Castillos Mountains and never encountered a single Apache along the way. Instead, they found the corpses of the slain Indians strewn across their home campground. Peacock walked among the bodies to discover if Juanita was among them. He could not find her.

Baylor met with Terrazas, who still camped nearby. Terrazas informed the Ranger captain that his soldiers had killed Victorio, but several of the captured Apaches claimed that the chief took his own life rather than be taken prisoner by the Mexicans. Baylor was also informed that more than a dozen Apaches managed to escape and flee north toward Texas. Minutes later, the captain had ordered his men to mount up and ride in pursuit. Baylor noted that the trail they followed led directly to the Eagle Mountains.

Days later, the Rangers entered the mountain range. Following the tracks of the Apaches, they encountered them a short time later and opened fire. The Indians took shelter behind nearby boulders. Taken by surprise, the Apaches were unprepared. As they ran for cover they grabbed their rifles but had no time to secure their bags of ammunition. For twenty-four hours the two groups exchanged gunfire before the Indians ran out of bullets. They were also desperately short on water and food.

Unaware that the Apaches had exhausted their supply of ammunition, Baylor ordered his men to hold their position and wait for a chance to attack. During the night, however, using only the illumination of a quarter moon, the Indians crept from the rocks and made their way past the Rangers and out of the Eagle Mountains. All night long they hiked and rode. The following day they reached the Sierra Diablo Mountains several miles to the north. They were ascending the foothills toward the higher elevations and another favored campsite with a spring when they were overtaken by the Rangers. A brief gun battle ensued, but the outnumbered and out-armed Indians had no chance. All were killed.

Following the skirmish, Peacock searched the faces of the victims trying to ascertain if Juanita was among them. She was not. For years, Peacock puzzled over what might have happened to the girl. He never saw her again.

More time passed, and Joe Peacock, now an old man, continued to raise cattle on his ranch not far from the Eagle Mountains. Though suffering from arthritis and finding it difficult to get around, he continued to return to the range to search for Victorio's lost cave of gold.

During one of his trips to the Eagle Mountains, Peacock encountered a young man named Race Compton. Compton, traveling on foot, had decided to spend some time in the range prospecting for ore. Compton invited Peacock to join him in his camp, and over the next few days the two men became friends and shared stories of their pasts. Peacock told Compton about his capture by the Apaches and learning about Chief Victorio's cave of gold. The two men decided to search for the cave together. Compton took up residence at Peacock's ranch. Enthused with having a partner to help him look for the gold, Peacock ignored his ranch as the two men spent more and more time in the mountain range. Peacock and Compton prowled the Eagle Mountains in search of the cave of gold for the next fifteen years. They never found it.

Joe Peacock died in 1915. Compton continued to live on Peacock's ranch while he pursued his search for the gold-filled cave. Compton raised a few head of cattle. From time to time he would sell one to raise money to purchase supplies for another foray into the mountains.

One day while Compton was in the mountain range, he was forced to lie up under a rock overhang for several hours during a heavy thunderstorm. When the clouds passed, Compton came out to continue his search. A short distance down the trail he noticed that runoff from the storm had washed away a portion of the rock debris on a particular slope. Climbing up to get a closer look, Compton came upon the outline of what appeared to be the entrance to a cave. After removing some of the covering debris, he found that the entrance had been closed off with heavy boulders. He labored for hours trying to remove them, but he lacked the strength to budge any but the smallest.

Compton decided to employ some men to remove the boulders, but then discarded the idea when he considered that, after seeing the store of gold inside, they might try to take it from him. Instead, he decided to travel to El Paso to procure some dynamite to blow the rocks out of the opening. On his way to El Paso, Compton mentioned his discovery to a neighboring rancher but offered no details regarding the location.

On his return trip, Compton hitched a ride from El Paso to Sierra Blanca, a small town several miles to the west of the Eagle Mountains. After being dropped off, he started walking along the highway. Some miles to the east, he knew he would come to a dirt road that would lead him into the Eagle Mountains. The knapsack he carried on his back was filled with sticks of dynamite he would use to open the cave. Compton was beginning to wonder what it was going to be like to be rich.

Race Compton never made it back to Victorio's cave. After hiking only a few miles out of Sierra Blanca, he suffered a heart attack and died. When he was found hours later, he was lying on the side of the road, his head resting on the knapsack filled with explosives.

Compton left no notes or maps regarding the location of the cave of gold. His few meager belongings were searched, as was the Peacock ranch house, but nothing of import was ever found. Compton owned nothing but the clothes on his back, a few cooking utensils, and a pistol that had not been fired in years.

Today, the Eagle Mountains can be seen by travelers motoring down U.S. Interstate 10 between Van Horn and Sierra Blanca. This rugged range is rarely visited except for a few hunters during deer season and an occasional rancher searching for cattle that may have strayed into one of the canyons. Near the old stagecoach station, the state of Texas has placed a historical marker containing only a few words.

The gold of Victorio, estimated to be worth an untold fortune, still lies concealed in a small cave somewhere in the range. From time to time, a treasure hunter will arrive in the area and conduct a search, but invariably comes away discouraged. This rugged, arid, harsh, rattlesnake-infested environment discourages all but the most determined and hardy adventurers.

19

THE LOST BILLY BOWLEGS TREASURE

The pirate William Rogers, who came to be known as Billy Bowlegs, was born in England. Part of his legend states that he was of noble blood but this has never been verified. Another part of the legend claims he was forced to flee his homeland because he was caught in a series of crooked business deals.

Whatever the truth, it is known for certain that he showed up in New Orleans, Louisiana, around 1810. He arrived with enough money to purchase a plantation seventy-five miles north of the Crescent City where he operated a profitable sugarcane farm. When asked about his origins and his past, Rogers remained very secretive and refused to divulge any information whatsoever. He eventually married a Choctaw woman who, over the years, provided him with four sons and two daughters.

William Rogers apparently tired of the tedium of farming and engaged in business with two men, Jean and Pierre Lafitte. The two Lafitte brothers made significant profits fencing the stolen goods that, as Rogers later learned, were plundered by the two men. Rogers eventually discovered that Jean Lafitte had his own fleet of pirate ships and raided and robbed across the Gulf of Mexico and the Atlantic Ocean. In 1812, Rogers joined up with Lafitte's band of brigands and participated in a number of raids. When Lafitte chose to join General Andrew "Old Hickory" Jackson's forces and fight against the British, Rogers did not hesitate to accompany him. He fought with valor at the Battle of New Orleans on January 8, 1815. As a result of his contributions, Rogers, along with Lafitte and several other crewmen, was granted a pardon by President James Madison for earlier crimes committed on the high seas.

When Lafitte shifted his pirating operation to Galveston Island in 1818, Rogers, reluctant to return to farming and attracted by the promise and potential for adventure and riches related to plundering merchant ships, remained behind and assembled his own fleet. For the next twenty-eight years, he was the scourge of the high seas. Somewhere along the way, Rogers acquired the nickname "Billy Bowlegs," the moniker taken from a Seminole Indian chief that Rogers resembled. The identity stuck, and before long no one could remember his real name. In fact, some have suggested that William Rogers may not have been an accurate identification.

From an unknown location somewhere on the Gulf Coast, Bowlegs and his fleet attacked and plundered Spanish ships throughout the area until 1838. All ships were fair prey for Bowlegs, regardless of their country of origin. He soon learned that Spanish vessels carried more gold and silver than those of France, England, or the United States. During that time, the Spanish normally carried precious metals and other valuable cargo from Mexico, South America, and Panama across the Atlantic Ocean to Spain. The so-called plate ships, so named because they were plated with sheets of metal that served as armor, were often escorted by one or more armed frigates to guard against depredation.

Most of the pirates prowling the Atlantic Ocean avoided the escorted treasure ships. Bowlegs, however, viewed them as a challenge, and attacked them with impunity. Every ship Bowlegs seized and plundered was either burned or scuttled after all of the crewmen were slain. The pirate wanted no survivors to return to shore and implicate him in his deeds.

By this time, Bowlegs and his compatriots were old men and the work of running ships and pillaging grew to be too much for them. Bowlegs retired, but after two years began to miss the thrill and adventure of piracy. In 1840, he reassembled several of his comrades along with some new crewmembers and returned to plundering merchant ships.

It has been rumored that Bowlegs had cached chests of pirate treasure in several different locations along the Gulf Coast, but the one that he is most associated with is a shipload of gold that went down in the shallow waters of Choctawhatchee Bay in the Florida Panhandle.

For one of his last raids, Bowlegs traveled to the Yucatan Peninsula in Mexico and robbed a pack train, along with a number of cargo wagons, of an immense fortune in gold. The account relates that Bowlegs had accumulated so much gold, tons of it, that he ordered the ship's cannons thrown overboard to allow for easier transportation of the loot.

On returning to his hideout on the Gulf Coast, Bowlegs encountered a storm. While he was fighting strong winds and high seas, he spotted a heavily armed British Man-of-War that had taken up pursuit of the pirate's vessel. Since Bowlegs had no cannons, he was defenseless. With his options limited, he attempted to outrun his pursuers.

By the time Bowlegs reached the Florida coast and the location of Camp Walton near Choctawhatchee Bay, the British were almost upon him. The pirate steered his vessel, the *Mysterio*, through East Pass and into the shallow bay, knowing that the Man-of-War's hull was too deep to pursue. As he sheltered in the bay, Bowlegs decided he would wait there until the British grew frustrated and sailed away.

Much to the pirate's surprise, however, the commander of the British ship lowered longboats filled with marines who continued the pursuit. Fearful that the British would confiscate his treasure, Bowlegs sailed his ship as close to Alaqua Bayou as he could, then scuttled it in the shallows. When the waters were up to the deck of the sinking ship, Bowlegs had the masts sawn off so the vessel would be totally submerged and not easily located. As the masts were being removed, Bowlegs had four cypress chests filled with gold and silver coins and jewels loaded into a rowboat and transported to the shore. As Bowlegs and his crew rowed and swam to safety, the ship, containing the bulk of his Mexican treasure, settled onto the sands below.

A short time later, the pirates stood along the shore and watched as the marines turned the longboats around and returned to the Man-of-War. When he was convinced they weren't being observed, Bowlegs and his crew unloaded the treasure chests from the rowboat and buried them nearby. After watching the British vessel sail away, Bowlegs decided to leave his crew at the location to guard the treasure while he set out overland for New Orleans where he hoped to obtain another ship and return with equipment to be used to retrieve the treasure in the sunken ship.

Bowlegs arrived at the bay a few weeks later in a small schooner. He brought along some diving equipment to assist in the recovery of the treasure. He also brought his wife and children. When Bowlegs arrived on the shore, he discovered that all but four of the crewmen he left near the bayou to guard his wealth had died of fever or Indian attack. The four survivors were weak and sickly and in no condition to help bring up the sunken treasure.

Bowlegs had a crude cabin constructed nearby. He was determined to wait for his men to recover from their sickness before undertaking a recovery operation. When they were well, Bowlegs intended to recruit others to assist him in bringing the treasure up from the bottom of the bay. A few weeks later, however, fever struck the area again, this time claiming additional crewmembers as well as Bowlegs's wife. Discouraged, the old pirate lost interest in the sunken treasure and began to believe it was cursed.

Years passed, and Bowlegs built a more substantial house not far from the point where the *Mysterio* sank. In time, Bowlegs was the only man left alive who knew the location of the scuttled treasure ship, as well as the four buried cypress chests filled with coins and jewels.

Bowlegs's children, having grown weary of living close to the edge of poverty, once approached the ex-pirate and requested he inform them of the locations of his buried treasures. Bowlegs refused, flew into a rage, and chased them away at the point of sword. For the rest of his life, he never revealed to them any of the secret locations of his buried caches.

For forty-eight years, Bowlegs lived more or less as a pauper even though he was only a short distance from several treasures. Before Bowlegs died at ninety-three years of age in 1888, he provided information on the location of the treasure ship, as well as where the four chests were buried, to a close friend and neighbor, a man named Moses Hudson.

A few months after Bowlegs died, Hudson found the sunken vessel. Unable to salvage the treasure by himself, he hired seven men to assist in the recovery. As the hired hands worked at trying to bring gold and silver up from the sunken ship, Hudson, in a moment of poor judgment, revealed to them the locations of the four cypress chests filled with gold and silver coins and indicated he also needed their help to dig them up. The far-too-trusting Hudson was double-crossed in a matter of days. The men dug up the chests and fled, leaving not a single coin for Hudson.

The deception caused Hudson to be more cautious. As a result, he never revealed the location of the sunken treasure ship to anyone again. For years, he kept the secret to himself. One day, however, he mentioned the site to his son, Ed. Ed, along with a friend, attempted to recover the treasure but had only a modicum of luck. They were able to locate a few gold coins in the area of the wreck, but the main treasure eluded them.

With the passage of more time, the story of the sunken treasure ship of Billy Bowlegs made the rounds throughout much of Florida. Strangers arrived in the region from time to time to try to find the sunken ship. One of the arrivals with a keen interest in recovering the pirate treasure was a retired physician named H. H. Humphreys. Humphreys spent weeks exploring various parts of Choctawhatchee Bay. With the aid of a Texas oil field engineer, Humphreys constructed a dam and partially drained the bay. At a point where Alaqua Creek forms a bayou that enters the bay, he found what he was convinced were the remains of the *Mysterio*.

The partially rotted vessel was seventy five feet long and held together with wooden pegs. Parts of the stern were visible but the rest of the ship was buried under a thick layer of silt. Humphreys's state-of-the-art detecting equipment found evidence of a quantity of dense metal beneath the sands but nothing was ever recovered except for an anchor chain. Given the comparatively primitive equipment available during that time, removing the sand and silt from the hulk of the wreck proved to be an insurmountable task.

Dedicated research leaves little doubt that the pirate Billy Bowlegs sank his ship, the *Mysterio*, with what is estimated to be in excess of sixty-five million dollars' worth of gold aboard. The remains of the ship have been found where Alaqua Bayou enters Choctawhatchee Bay. It is possible, with modern recovery equipment, that the pirate's long-lost treasure could be recovered. It would require a significant investment in time, energy, and money to do so, but finding the huge quantity of gold would make the effort worthwhile.

20

GASPARILLA'S LOST TREASURE

D on Jose Gaspar, better known as the pirate Gasparilla, was responsible for the sinking of a ship carrying millions of dollars' worth
of gold and silver coins and ingots, as well as other treasures. The event
took place in the shallow waters of Boca Grande Pass, an entrance to
Charlotte Harbor in Charlotte County on the southwestern side of
Florida. It is believed that Gasparilla was transporting well over a million dollars' worth of booty at the time, a value that translates into an
unimaginable fortune today

Unlike many of the sunken treasure ships associated with the
state of Florida, Gasparilla's vessel, also named *Gasparilla*, has received
comparatively little attention. Some have suggested that this is because
Gasparilla was not as well known or as colorful as other pirates who frequented the Atlantic and Gulf waters, brigands such as Blackbeard and
Lafitte. Regardless, Gasparilla was just as successful as the others, if not
more, and the treasure he left behind is no less impressive and continues
to tempt fortune hunters.

Born Don Jose Gaspar in Spain in 1756, he made the decision as a
young boy that he was made for a life on the sea. At fifteen, he joined
the king's navy. Because he was from a poor family, he was ineligible
for the position of officer and served as an enlisted man for seven years.
In that capacity, however, Gaspar proved to be a competent seaman and
fearless in battle. While only a midshipman, he was awarded knighthood
by the king of Spain. When he turned twenty-two years of age he was
given captaincy of a warship and ordered to the Caribbean. Within five
years he distinguished himself so well that he was returned to Spain to

serve as an advisor to the king. By this time he was married and had a child.

While he was serving as a court advisor, the queen attempted to seduce him. When he refused her advances, she was insulted. The vindictive queen vowed revenge for the offense to her pride and ordered Gaspar's wife and child, along with his mother, killed. On receiving the news of the brutal murders, Gaspar swore revenge and thereafter became a bitter enemy of Spain and its rulers.

One night, after enlisting help from a few close friends, Gaspar stormed a prison, killed the guards, and released all of the prisoners. From the newly freed men he organized a ship's crew. The following week, Gaspar, along with his crewmen, stole one of the king's warships. He set sail immediately for the West Indies, where he recruited more men, good seaman and fighters all, and then headed for Florida to establish a headquarters.

When Gasparilla was plying his trade as pirate during the late 1700s, life for such adventurers on the high seas was considerably more difficult that it was for those who came before him decades earlier. Now, pirate vessels were regularly hunted down by ships flying the flags of England, the United States, France, and Spain. A number of pirate strongholds along the Atlantic and Gulf coasts, as well as in the Caribbean Islands, were attacked and cleaned out one by one, with the brigands fleeing from the invaders, never to return. These bases of operations were important to the pirates. From there they obtained supplies and often disposed of much of the loot and merchandise they had captured. Furthermore, they were locations where the pirates could rest and relax after months at sea and conduct repairs and maintenance on the ships.

Gasparilla chose to operate one such base on the west coast of the Florida mainland, at the time a Spanish territory. This location, now known as Charlotte Harbor near Port Charlotte and Fort Myers, was seldom visited by warships of other countries, and it afforded a sheltered location with a deep-water harbor. The entrance was hidden from all but the most experienced sailors. It was also easy to defend should the need arise.

At this location, Gasparilla founded a town called Alta Puebla. It was located at the end of a long, narrow peninsula and at the entrance to the harbor. Today, it is known as Boca Grande. Here Gasparilla made his headquarters, often shared with other sea-going cutthroats including Caesar LeGrande (known as Black Caesar) and Brewster Baker (known as Brubaker), as well as others. This loosely organized band of pirates referred to themselves as "The Brotherhood of the Seas," and often conducted raids together, always with Gasparilla in command.

For years, Gasparilla and his companions ranged out from the stronghold to raid and plunder, attacking ships, sacking and looting coastal towns, and occasionally taking prisoners they held for ransom. While any and all merchant vessels were considered fair game for the pirate, Gasparilla took great pleasure in seizing ships belonging to Spain.

In time, Gasparilla and his gang established trading centers along the coast and on a few islands where they dealt goods to mainland merchants. They even carried merchandise and contraband to larger cities such as New Orleans.

In 1819, the United States acquired Florida from Spain. One of the first major decisions made regarding this new territory was to rid the region of pirates once and for all. The federal government established the U.S. Revenue Service, a forerunner to the Coast Guard. The U.S.R.S. operated in conjunction with the U.S. Navy, and armed ships were occasionally sent out to eliminate the pirate menace from the Gulf of Mexico. A fleet under the command of Commodore David Porter was ordered to capture or kill all pirate crews they encountered.

Gasparilla learned of the approaching Revenue Service warships and realized he was about to be outnumbered and outgunned. He decided he did not want to tangle with them. Instead, he decided it was time to depart Charlotte Harbor and find a better location from which to conduct his piratical operations. He considered Central or South America. During the time he had before sailing away, the pirate leader converted all of his wealth into gold coins and jewels and had them loaded aboard his ship, the *Gasparilla*. His treasure was estimated to be worth well over one million dollars at the time, an immense fortune.

As he was preparing the flagship for departure, one of his crewmembers informed him that a ship was positioned just outside the entrance to the harbor at Boca Grande Pass. After examining the vessel through his telescope, Gasparilla decided it was a trading vessel and that he would seize it, along with whatever goods and treasure it carried, before leaving the area.

Unknown to the pirate leader, the ship was the U.S.S. *Enterprise,* camouflaged to look like a merchant ship. As the *Gasparilla* closed in on the stationary vessel, Commodore Porter brought his cannons to the fore and ordered a bombardment. Too late, the pirate leader realized his mistake. In less than five minutes, the *Gasparilla* was riddled with cannon shot and sinking. A few minutes later it settled onto the bottom sands in the mouth of Boca Grande Pass.

Today there remains some small amount of controversy regarding the sinking of the *Gasparilla.* While most researchers maintain that the vessel was destroyed from cannon fire, others suggest that Gasparilla himself ordered the ship scuttled so that his treasure could not be seized.

In addition, there exists controversy over the manner in which Gasparilla died. Many researchers claim he simply went down with his ship. Another source, however, claims the pirate wrapped a length of anchor chain around his waist and jumped overboard to his death.

The ship's crew that did not drown managed to swim to nearby La Costa Island on the south side of the pass. They were immediately captured or killed by troopers from the U.S.S. *Enterprise.*

✦

Although the location of the long-sunken *Gasparilla* is known, aside from a handful of unsuccessful freelance recovery efforts, not a single organized attempt has been made to retrieve the treasure that went down with it. Other sunken treasures up and down the east and west coasts of Florida have attracted a number of professional treasure hunters, but the *Gasparilla* remains relatively untouched. In the years that have passed since the sinking, coins from its cargo have been found washed up on nearby beaches following storms.

In addition to Gasparilla's gold and silver, there is even more reason for treasure hunters to reach the cargo transported by the *Gasparilla.* Research has revealed that among the treasure being transported by Gasparilla was a quantity of U.S. silver dollars minted between 1799 and 1804. These coins were in favor with the pirates when conducting business on the mainland. They are extremely rare and the collector value is immense.

21

COLONEL DUNHAM'S
LOST PAYROLL

During the Civil War, both Yankee and Confederate forces remained constantly on the move throughout selected portions of the American South. The state of Tennessee saw as much traffic as any other. Along with men, horses, mules, artillery, wagons, supplies, and more, the armies of the North and South carried payrolls. Payment, both in currency and coin, was passed out at the end of the month to the soldiers while on the march. It is estimated that at any given time during the war, payrolls amounting to millions of dollars were in transit from one skirmish to another, from one campsite to another.

In December of 1862, Union Colonel C. L. Dunham, commander of the 39th Iowa Division, led mounted troops and foot soldiers into western Tennessee with the intention of engaging Confederate General Nathan Bedford Forrest and his Seventh Tennessee Cavalry. On December 29th, Dunham's division, heading south, passed through the small Carroll County town of Huntington in the western part of the state.

Dunham was a newcomer in the territory with which Forrest was highly experienced. The Confederate general had considerable success in battles and skirmishes throughout that part of Tennessee. Dunham's most recent intelligence had Forrest's army camped at a location called Parker's Crossroads, located fifteen miles south of Huntington. Dunham received specific orders from General Ulysses S. Grant to proceed to Forrest's location, engage, and defeat the enemy. Forrest and his army had created a great deal of trouble and embarrassment for the Union forces in West Tennessee, and Grant wanted to put an end to it.

By the time Dunham's command reached Clarksburg, ten miles south of Huntington, the sun had set. A few hundred yards out of town, one of the scouts found a freshwater spring and a suitable place to establish a camp for the night. Dunham directed his troopers toward the location, known locally as Dollar Hill, and within minutes tents were set up, horses and mules were unsaddled and hobbled, cooking fires were started, and guards were posted around the perimeter.

During the night, Dunham's scouts were sent forward to ascertain Forrest's exact location and the number of Rebel troops under his command. Reporting back just before dawn of the following day, the scouts informed the colonel that the Confederate command was, indeed, camped at Parker's Crossroads five miles away and due south. The Rebels were apparently aware of Dunham's approaching Union force, for they were spotted digging trenches and making other battle preparations.

Without taking time for breakfast, Dunham ordered his soldiers to ready their weapons and mounts for the march to Forrest's camp. As the troopers busied themselves with preparations for the coming battle, Dunham addressed the disposition of the payroll chest. Not wishing to risk its capture by the Confederate forces, Parker decided to bury it. The chest contained fifteen thousand dollars in coins. When the battle was over and the Union forces victorious, Dunham intended to return to the campsite and retrieve the payroll. With the aid of two trusted lieutenants and one sergeant, Dunham and his men alternately carried and dragged the heavy chest to a location two hundred feet east of the spring. Here a shallow hole was excavated, the chest lowered into it, and then covered over.

Unseen by the four men, a Union scout named Allen Chambliss was squatted on a low knoll overlooking the excavation site. As he smoked a cigarette and cleaned his rifle, Chambliss observed the caching of the payroll chest. Chambliss sat quietly throughout the process, not wishing to be seen. This made a total of five men who had knowledge of the location of the buried coins.

For most of the day, Dunham's command advanced slowly and cautiously toward the Confederate encampment, taking extreme care to keep silent and unseen. By nightfall, the Yankees, hiding in the woods, could see the campfires in the distance. Men in Confederate uniforms were spotted moving about a few hundred yards away. Not wishing to engage the well-entrenched enemy in the dark, the members of the 39th Iowa Division fought for whatever sleep they could get, readying themselves for a strike on the Rebel camp at dawn.

Moments before sunrise on the morning of December 31, the first shots were fired from the Yankees in hiding and the fight was on. For nearly a full day, the two sides exchanged gunfire with both incurring heavy casualties. Dunham's command outnumbered the Confederates by a significant margin, but the canny Forrest managed to create mass confusion and heavy damage. Late in the day, and having accomplished all he believed was possible against Dunham's superior numbers, Forrest ordered his soldiers to retreat southeastward from the battle site. A short time later, they crossed the Tennessee River near the town of Clifton and proceeded on toward Lawrenceburg a few miles north of the Alabama border.

At the Parker's Crossroads battle site, nearly one hundred men, both Union and Confederate, lay dead. Hundreds more had suffered serious wounds, and during the next several days and nights, military surgeons treated the injured while squads of enlisted men buried the dead. Dunham looked on as the two lieutenants and the sergeant who helped him bury the payroll chest were lowered into the ground.

The tasks of treating the injured and burying the dead were not made any easier by the heavy rains that began to fall on the morning after the battle. The downpour lasted for seven days. Between the cold and the rain, conditions became intolerable for the troopers. Because it was impossible to maintain cooking fires, the soldiers were forced to eat cold rations or none at all.

Among the Union soldiers recovering from wounds in one of the army tents was Allen Chambliss. He had been struck by a Rebel bullet during the first few minutes of the action, lost a great deal of blood, and was initially pronounced dead. On the third day after the battle he regained consciousness, and the doctors believed his chances for a full recovery were good.

As Chambliss lay on his cot being tended to by medical aides, the battlefield had turned into a quagmire and movement was restricted. On the morning of the sixth day, Colonel Dunham assembled a contingent of six well-armed men, appropriated a stout wagon, and rode back toward Clarksburg with the intention of retrieving the payroll chest.

On two occasions Dunham and his soldiers were forced to abandon the trail and take to the deep woods in order to hide from Rebel patrols. When they had finally reached a point two miles from their goal, they were fired upon by a third enemy patrol and two of the Union soldiers were killed. Finally, frustrated by the weather and the threat of Confederates in the area, Dunham decided to abandon the chest for the time being.

When the rain finally let up, Dunham led his command back toward the north where he hoped to find a suitable place to rest men and horses and replenish supplies. Several of the most seriously wounded soldiers, including Chambliss, were taken to a makeshift hospital in Huntington to recover. While waiting in the town, Dunham received orders to assemble all of his able-bodied soldiers and head an expedition into another region in Tennessee. With the formidable task of leading men into battle and securing victory for the North, Dunham eventually forgot about the buried payroll chest located near the spring outside the town of Clarksburg. While recovering in the hospital, Chambliss could think of nothing but the buried treasure, and he made plans to retrieve it as soon as he was released.

Three months passed before Chambliss recovered sufficiently from his wound to leave the hospital. Deciding not to rejoin his unit, the scout obtained a mount and rode south toward Clarksburg. His intention was to retrieve the payroll chest and return to his farm a much richer man than when he left.

On arriving, Chambliss was surprised to discover that the landscape surrounding the spring had changed dramatically. Heavy runoff from the torrential rains that had plagued Dunham's command for a full week had filled the nearby streams, creating flash floods and severe erosion. The increased overland runoff had carried away tons of topsoil in some areas and deposited it in others. It was with difficulty that Chambliss finally found what he believed was the actual location of the spring near where the Union soldiers had camped before engaging Forrest. He tied his horse to a bush and walked over to the spot where he was convinced the chest had been buried. Employing a long, thin metal stick known as a punch rod, Chambliss plunged it into the soft ground here and there in hope of locating the cache. Having no success with this procedure, he excavated a wide hole at a site he was certain was the correct one, but nothing was found. Chambliss dug in another location with the same result. By the end of the day, at least a dozen holes had been dug but the payroll chest remained elusive.

For several months, Chambliss camped near the spring and searched the area over and over for the buried chest, but with no success. On several occasions he would walk to the low hill from which he had observed the burial of the chest, but from his vantage point nothing looked the same as it did before the heavy rains.

Over the years, Chambliss related the story of his search for the buried payroll chest, and in time the tale entered the annals of Tennessee folklore. One of the men who heard of Chambliss's experience was the late Gray Roark, a resident of Huntington. On at least a couple of occasions, Roark attempted to locate the buried payroll but had no more success than Chambliss. Years passed, and Roark related the story of Chambliss's search for the gold to his step-grandson, J. E. Bates, who has kept the story of the lost payroll alive.

A search of government records revealed that Dunham did, in fact, transport a payroll chest during his mission to engage General Forrest. What became of it was not recorded. When Dunham's personal journal was located, it was searched for information pertaining to the burying of the payroll chest, but no mention of the event was ever found. Because the busy commander had little time for making notations in his journal, he likewise made no mention of the routes he traveled or the locations of campsites.

In spite of the fact that the Union payroll chest was buried a century and a half ago, people continue to search for it. To compound the difficulty in finding the chest, researchers have discovered there is not just one spring located in this area, but as many as five. Which of the springs was the one near where Dunham buried the payroll chest remains a mystery, one that has attracted the analysis of many, including Civil War enthusiasts, treasure hunters, historians, archeologists, and others, all of whom have expressed different reasons for wanting to locate and recover the lost Yankee payroll.

22

CUMBERLAND MOUNTAIN
SILVER MINES

The Cumberland Mountains of east-central Tennessee have long been a puzzle to geologists. Most of their research over the years suggests that the rock structure and composition of the range is unlikely to produce precious metals. In spite of these authoritative declarations, however, tales have long persisted that the mining of silver has taken place in these mountains. The truth is, documents exist proving that silver has been mined and processed in the Tennessee Appalachians and the ore has been seen and handled by a number of people.

While the findings of qualified geologists are often important and useful to treasure hunters in search of lost mines, it must be pointed out that they have been proven wrong many times in the past. Furthermore, the regional legend and lore, though scoffed at by the so-called intellectual elite, have proven true in many cases.

The Cumberland Mountains had been occupied by the Cherokee Indians for many generations before the arrival of white men in the region. Among the variety of jewelry and ornamentation worn by the Cherokee were a number of items fashioned from silver. The ore, the Indians explained to some of the early trappers who came to this region, was dug from several mines located in the Cumberland range.

One particular tale that has been retold many times tells of a small party of Cherokee arriving at the Piney Creek region of the Cumberlands during the late 1860s. They had traveled from Indian Territory (now Oklahoma), and their long, slow journey had taken several weeks. During a period of federally mandated displacement twenty years earlier, the Indians had been forced to leave the Cumberland range and were sent to live on reservations. Now, riding in two stout wagons pulled by mules, the Cherokee arrived at their old Piney Creek homeland and set up a crude temporary camp. Prior to leaving two decades before, the tribe elders had covered up the entrances to the silver mines and had buried a quantity of silver in the form of ornaments, jewelry, and nuggets not far from Piney Creek. They always knew that someday they would return.

During the day, the Cherokee encampment remained quiet and the occupants kept to themselves. When curious residents dropped by to inquire about their business, the Indians were polite and explained that they were only traveling and needed to rest their stock for a few days.

At night, however, the Indians invested a great deal of time and labor reopening some of the mines and harvesting more of the ore. They also dug up some of the silver from the many caches located nearby. After all of the ore was accumulated back at the camp, it was loaded into the wagons and covered with tarps and camping gear. Several days later when they departed, area residents noted that the deep wheel ruts left by the wagons suggested they were transporting heavy loads of some kind. The residents, all of whom had heard the stories of the Cherokee silver mines, speculated that the Indians had recovered some of their wealth to take back to Oklahoma. Several of the Piney Creek residents tried to backtrack the wagons to the campsite and range out in an attempt to locate the mines or a treasure cache, but they had no success.

During the 1870s, a Piney Creek area old-timer named Leffew was long intrigued by the tales of the secret Cherokee silver mines. Leffew lived with his wife and children deep in the Cumberland Mountains and as far from neighbors as he could get. He survived as a farmer, making a sparse living for his family raising hogs and chickens and growing corn on a hardscrabble ridge top, part of the Cumberland Escarpment, near a tiny community called Concord Church a few miles from Spring City.

Leffew has been described as a tall, gaunt man with large hands calloused by years of hard work in the out of doors. His skin was leathery and tanned and he always seemed in need of a bath and shave. Those who chanced to visit the Leffew farm described it as poor and suffering from neglect. The unchinked log cabin allowed the freezing air of deep winter to penetrate.

Leffew's neighbors avoided him at every turn, thinking him peculiar and perhaps dangerous. They were always uncomfortable when he happened by. The few times Leffew ventured into nearby settlements, he was generally avoided. The farmer was often spotted walking alone and talking to himself, gesturing animatedly, and sometimes screaming at demons only he could see. Leffew also suffered from a severe nervous tic that caused his left shoulder to jerk sharply forward every few seconds. The movements suggested a grotesque dance and lent a bizarre touch to an already odd character.

Sometime during the first part of the 1870s, Leffew began neglecting his farm and family more than usual. He often disappeared for days at a time into the dark and gloomy canyons that held tributaries to Piney Creek. His frequent and extended trips away from home began to worry his wife and children.

One day, after having been gone for a week, Leffew arrived at the front door of his cabin and informed his wife that he had found a silver mine deep in Piney Creek gorge. From a filthy leather pouch that hung from his scrawny neck, Leffew pulled a large nugget of almost pure silver and held it up as proof.

The following day, Leffew took his silver nugget into Spring City and displayed it to any and all who cared to see it. In a fit of behavior rather uncharacteristic for the eccentric old farmer, Leffew bought several rounds of drinks for everyone at a local tavern.

In a very short time, Leffew, who rarely drank alcohol at all, was feeling the effects of the liquor. Uncommonly proud of what he called his newfound silver mine, he boasted loud and long that he would soon be a rich man. During his bragging, Leffew let it slip that the mine was located in the Piney Creek gorge and not far from a prominent and well-known landmark known locally as Big Rock.

Leffew's announcement had, for him, an undesired effect. Several men who were at the bar and heard his story began searching for the mine at the first opportunity. Each time Leffew left his cabin and entered the woods in the Piney Creek area, he was followed by men who waited in hiding for him to leave. Aware of his trackers, and somewhat wise in the ways of the wild, he always managed to elude them. For several months, men attempted to trail Leffew to his secret mine but always failed.

One afternoon, a young black man appeared at the mercantile in Sheffield (now called Evensville), twelve miles southwest of Spring City. He told the owner that a man named Leffew had hired him to help dig some silver ore out of a mine, and had sent him to town to purchase some dynamite and mining supplies. Following the purchase, which was paid for with silver ore, the man loaded the items onto two mules and led the animals out of town back toward Piney Creek. It was the last time anyone saw him alive.

A few weeks later the partially decomposed body of the black man was found on the bank of Piney Creek near a point where it was joined by one of its tributaries. The man had been shot through the head. Though few cared to speculate, most were convinced that Leffew had killed the young fellow to prevent him from revealing the location of the silver mine. To this day, the small narrow canyon located near where the body was found is known as Dead Negro Hollow.

A few months passed, and it was noted that a gang of tough-looking men began hanging around the Leffew farm. It was clear to all who happened to pass by that Leffew was not in favor of the company of these desperate-looking characters and would caution his wife and children to remain in the cabin while he met with them in the woods. Though Leffew's wife asked him several times who the men were, he never provided an answer.

Before long, it leaked out that the men staying at Leffew's farm were part of a gang of counterfeiters who allegedly manufactured phony silver coins at a secret location in the mountains. A number of towns-people suspected Leffew had become part of the gang, perhaps unwillingly, and was supplying the silver from his secret mine for the coins.

One afternoon as Leffew was leaving his house on his way to the mine, he was met in the yard by a group of men Mrs. Leffew described as members of the counterfeit gang. Watching from the window, Mrs. Leffew saw an argument break out between her husband and one of the men. A short time later, the farmer told his wife he was going to his silver mine and would return the following day. When two days had passed and Leffew did not show up, the wife approached neighbors and requested their help to search for him. Another day went by and there was no sign of Leffew. The sheriff was summoned and he organized yet another search. After a week of combing the woods looking for Leffew, it was called off.

A year passed before it could be determined what happened to Leffew. One day, three young boys were hunting raccoons near Vinegar Hill when they made a grisly discovery. Hanging from the limb of a tree was the desiccated body of a man. The dried-out corpse was dangling from leather suspenders that had been wrapped tightly around its neck. Clothing, boots, and other items found nearby suggested the skeleton belonged to Leffew.

Some speculated that Leffew, harboring guilt over the killing of the young black man, committed suicide. Most who knew the farmer, however, claimed such a thing was not in his nature, and that he was likely killed by the men he had an argument with on the day he disappeared.

Several more years passed. One afternoon, a local farmer named Thurmond was out searching for stray cattle in the Piney Creek gorge. While climbing a steep wall of the canyon, he found an opening in the rock just wide enough to allow passage of a man. A pile of tailings outside the opening suggested to Thurmond that some excavation had taken place. Thurmond had heard stories of the lost silver mines in the area but never believed any of them. He wondered if he had accidentally discovered one of them.

Pressed for time, Thurmond continued looking for his cattle, intending to return later and investigate the mine. The continual duties of running a farm, however, kept him busy for the next several weeks. When he finally found some time to devote to a return to the mine, he was unable to locate it. For years, he tried to return to the mysterious shaft in the side of the canyon but it always eluded him.

During the 1920s, a Tennessee man named Warrick had heard all of the tales about the lost Cherokee silver mines in the Cumberland Mountains. He was also familiar with the story of farmer Leffew's lost silver mine. Warrick decided there was enough evidence to suggest that such a mine, or mines, did exist and he decided to undertake a search. Warrick had lived in the region all of his life and was related to a number of people. Throughout the years, he had entered the Piney Creek gorge on several occasions while hunting and was very familiar with it.

For months, Warrick searched in the gorge, always remaining optimistic that he would encounter the silver mine at any moment. Late one afternoon, a tired and sweat-grimed Warrick walked into the home of his sister and announced to her that he had discovered the mine.

Each day for several weeks thereafter, Warrick traveled to Piney Creek and dug out a handful of silver ore. Each evening on his way to his own home, he would stop at his sister's house to relate the day's activities. The sister always insisted on seeing some of the ore that Warrick claimed he retrieved, but he steadfastly refused to show it to her for reasons he never explained. After weeks of the same response, she finally accused Warrick of fabricating the tale of his discovery.

One Sunday as Warrick and his sister were walking home from church, he told her he wanted to show her something. He led her several yards off the trail near a point called Warrick Fork and pointed to a large boulder. With some difficulty, Warrick rolled the rock aside, revealing a shallow hole. Inside the hole, according to the sister, were several leather pouches, each one filled with silver nuggets.

Warrick explained to his sister that this was where he cached all of the silver he dug from the mine and that he added to it each time he returned from the mine with more of the ore. He said that if anything ever happened to him, he wanted her to have his fortune. She apologized for doubting his word and the two proceeded on down the trail.

Months passed, and Warrick continued to harvest silver from the secret mine and cache it beneath the large boulder. One morning, like so many others, he gathered up his digging tools and headed down the trail toward Piney Creek gorge. As he passed his sister's house, he called out a greeting as he walked by. She waved back. It was the last time anyone ever saw Warrick.

Warrick's fate was never learned. When he did not return from the mine in a reasonable time, his sister organized a search for him. He was never found. Some have suggested he may have met with foul play, perhaps murdered by someone who wanted to learn the location of the mine. Others suggest Warrick simply left the country. Evidence for the latter came when the sister and another relative went to the large boulder, rolled it aside, and found the hole where Warrick cached his silver empty. The disappearance of Warrick remains a mystery to this day.

The area around Spring City in the Cumberland Mountains is not much different today than it was when farmer Leffew lived and farmed there during the late 1800s. The region remains thinly populated and heavily forested. Hikers and hunters who travel to Piney Creek gorge must deal with rattlesnakes and ticks. The remains of old moonshine stills in the narrow canyons and shallow caves can still be found.

In spite of the somewhat rugged and forbidding environment, occasional treasure hunters arrive in the area of the Cumberland Escarpment to search for Leffew's silver mine, as well as for the lost silver mines of the Cherokee Indians. The area can tax the conditioning and endurance of any who come to search the woods, the gorges, and the ridge tops. The reward of locating the mine or any of the related caches, however, could make the effort worthwhile.

23

DEVIL'S CANYON GOLD

Devil's Canyon is located at the extreme western end of the Wichita Mountain range of Oklahoma. It is a southwest–northeast cut in the rock flanked by Flat Top Mountain and Soldiers' Peak. The steep walls of the two mountains keep much of the canyon in shade during the day, lending a dark and forbidding atmosphere to the rocky, brush-choked floor of the gorge.

There are legends associated with Devil's Canyon. One of them relates that the place has long been haunted by the spirits of the many men who died there. Indeed, during the past two centuries, dozens of skeletons have been found in this location, along with bits and pieces of Spanish armor and mining gear. An abundance of Indian artifacts have also been found, suggesting a large Comanche encampment was once located near the mouth of the canyon.

Another legend is related to lost treasure. The Wichita Mountains are made up of rugged intrusive rock outcrops that originated millions of years ago as a result of deep and violent underground volcanic activity. The very forces that gave rise to these huge granite structures are the same ones associated with the formation of gold and silver, both of which are found in the range. During the early part of the seventeenth century, the Spanish invested a great deal of time exploring this region and attempting to establish a settlement. While their colonization efforts failed, their mining activities succeeded, and legends describe the great wealth in gold and silver mined and shipped back to Mexico City headquarters or across the Atlantic Ocean to Spain.

Devil's Canyon was the site of a Spanish mission established in 1629 by Padre Juan de Salas. De Salas, along with a few Indian converts to Christianity, attempted to grow corn and beans near the mouth of the canyon, where a small stream empties into the North Fork of the Red River. The tiny settlement languished for years, and then was abandoned in response to a prolonged drought.

More Spanish arrived at Devil's Canyon again in 1650. This time it was a small detachment of the army led by Captain Hernán Martín and adventurer Don Diego del Castillo. The party searched for gold and silver and, encouraged by discoveries of the ore, reported their findings to their superiors.

In 1657, a Spanish priest named Gilbert arrived at Devil's Canyon with a group of one hundred men. Employing directions provided by Martín and del Castillo, they located the gold deposits and began mining. A deep shaft—over one hundred feet—was sunk into the solid granite of the canyon floor. Several mule loads of ore were dug from the mine, but the area was abandoned because of the continued and growing threat of hostile Indians.

In 1698, a party of Spaniards disembarked at a port near New Orleans and undertook the long journey from the Gulf Coast to the Wichita Mountains. The expedition consisted of one hundred men equipped with mining tools along with a detachment of fifty soldiers. While the laborers and engineers dug the gold from the shaft, the soldiers tried to keep the threat of raiding Indians to a minimum. Following a set of maps and charts, the Spaniards reached Devil's Canyon after a journey of several weeks. Once there, they established a permanent camp, constructed several dwellings of adobe and rock, and a church. In a nearby rock shelter they built a primitive smelter.

Time passed, and as the Spaniards mined and smelted the ore, the canyon was visited on occasion by Indians. At first, the visits were hostile, but when it became clear that the newcomers were only interested in the shiny colored rock they dug from the ground, a kind of truce was established and the Indians lost interest in them.

Two to three times each year, a mule train loaded with gold ingots would depart from Devil's Canyon and proceed to the port on the Gulf. There, the gold was loaded onto a ship and carried across the ocean to Spain. The Spaniards would rest a few days in the growing city, purchase supplies and equipment, and make the long journey back to the Wichita Mountains.

As the years wore on, the relations between the miners and the Indians grew tense. Though the Indians cared little about the Spaniards' activities in the canyon, they resented the impact the Europeans had on the game in the region. From time to time, hunting parties consisting of soldiers would be sent out to secure meat for the settlement. With each trip, they were forced to range farther afield because of the ongoing depletion of the herds of bison, deer, and antelope.

During some of these hunting expeditions, the soldiers were attacked by the Indians, and a few Spaniards were killed. When entire hunting parties failed to return, it was presumed they were slaughtered by the Indians. The Spaniards found it necessary to post guards around the settlement day and night. By day, the Spaniards could see Indians standing along the ridge tops observing them at their work.

Early one winter morning, a pack train consisting of fifty mules, each carrying a heavy load of gold, departed the canyon and headed southeastward toward the Gulf. As the last mule passed through the mouth of the canyon, the Spaniards were attacked by what was later estimated to be more than two hundred mounted warriors. As the armed escort attempted to fight off the Indians, miners and soldiers from the settlement raced to the scene to assist their comrades. The result was inevitable, however, for within an hour all of the Spaniards lay dead save for three who escaped.

The area in and around Devil's Canyon remained quiet for a time. The only visitors were small hunting parties. In 1765, a French explorer named Brevel arrived in the area and made friends with the Indians who related the story of the slaughter of the Spaniards almost a century earlier. Brevel visited Devil's Canyon and noted the remains of the mining and smelting activity as well as the ruins of the old church and dwellings. He recorded his observations in his journal.

During the next several years, travelers and explorers to the region reported spotting the crumbling ruins of the Spanish structures and the remains of the mining activity. Despite the presence of gold, no one attempted to reopen the mines. During the 1830s, a party of Mexicans moved into the canyon and set up residence. A prevalent legend says that the Mexicans were led by a descendant of one of the survivors of the massacre that had occurred decades earlier. Carrying maps and descriptions of the great wealth to be found in Devil's Canyon, they located and reopened the mines.

In 1833, a man named Simon N. Cockrell, a scout for some businessmen who wanted to establish a trading post in the region, visited the canyon and observed the Mexicans hard at work in the mines. He reported that, though the Mexicans were friendly enough, they remained somewhat secretive relative to the mining activities.

During the summer of 1834, the Mexicans were preparing to leave Devil's Canyon with several dozen mule loads of gold ore when they were set upon by a band of Kiowa Indians. A fierce battle erupted at the mouth of the canyon. Several of the Mexicans rushed to the gold mine and struggled to cover the entrance with large boulders. This done, they returned to the scene of the battle to aid their fellows. By the time they arrived, however, the fight was over and the Kiowa victorious. As the Indians went from body to body taking scalps, the surviving Mexicans concealed themselves among the boulders along one of the canyon walls and waited for the chance to escape.

Finished with scalping and mutilating the bodies, the Indians turned the pack train back into the canyon where they unloaded all of the ore, cached it in a cave in one canyon wall, and covered the entrance with several tons of rock and debris. Rounding up all of the now unburdened mules, the Indians left the canyon. When they thought it was safe, the Mexicans who were in hiding came forth and set out on foot for Mexico where months later they reported the massacre.

In 1850 a second group of Mexicans arrived at Devil's Canyon. Smaller than the earlier group, this one was led by one of the men who had escaped the attack by the Kiowa Indians sixteen years earlier. On first entering the canyon, the Mexicans set up camp near a small pool of water just beyond the entrance. On the morning of the second day, they walked to the place where the Kiowa had cached the gold ore after the massacre. As the men labored to remove the rocks covering the cave, two young boys were sent to the trading post seven miles up the North Fork of the Red River to purchase some supplies. When the boys had traveled one-half mile after leaving the canyon, they heard gunfire and screams coming from where their comrades had been digging. Racing their horses back into the canyon, they spotted a large band of Indians attacking the party. The boys turned their mounts and rode for the trading post in hope of recruiting some help. Later, when they returned with a group of ten men, they discovered all of their companions had been killed and scalped.

The Wichita Mountains have been claimed as home territory by numerous Indian tribes, including Comanche, Kiowa, and Wichita, all of which found the abundant game and water to their liking and perceived the rugged vastness as easy to defend against encroaching white settlers.

Anglo settlement and ranching in and around the Wichita Mountains began during the mid-nineteenth century. By 1880, several large and successful ranches had been established. The area came under the protection of the U.S. Army; several companies of well-mounted and well-armed cavalry were stationed in the region to guard the whites against Indian depredations.

During the early 1870s, a man named J. C. Settles established a large ranch near Devil's Canyon. From time to time while tending his cattle, Settles would ride into the canyon. There he spotted the remains of the old Spanish church and dwellings. Settles had heard tales of gold being mined from the canyon but did not believe them.

Settles made friends with many of the Indians who remained in the area and often hired some of them to work on his ranch. One afternoon Settles and an elderly Kiowa were running some cattle toward a pond in Devil's Canyon when the Indian related the story of the massacre of the Mexicans many years earlier. He also told Settles that he knew of a place back in the canyon where the Mexicans mined the ore and could take him to it. He told Settles that the miners had excavated a shaft over one hundred feet deep straight down into the solid rock of the canyon floor. He also explained how the Mexicans rolled large boulders over the opening to conceal it.

Though Settles was intrigued with this story, he was far too busy working his cattle ranch to take time off to investigate the old mine. Several years later, however, he invested some time and energy in a search. He located an ancient shaft that had been partially covered by a large boulder. With difficulty, he succeeded in blasting it from the opening. Inside the shaft, Settles found a human skeleton and what he described as a "coal-like substance" he couldn't identify. Without having any of the rock from the shaft assayed, Settles abandoned the mine, never to return.

In 1900, an aged Kiowa woman was seen hiking near Devil's Canyon. Those who saw her said it appeared as though she were searching for something. When questioned, the woman claimed that, as a young girl, she had accompanied the band of Kiowas that attacked and killed the Mexican miners in 1834. She said she had helped two warriors hide three mule loads of gold after the battle and she was now searching for them. Though the woman remained in the area for two weeks, she never found the cache.

In the years immediately after 1900, there was a spate of prospecting and mining activity in the Wichita Mountains. A number of entrepreneurs, geologists, engineers, and investors studied the prospects of Devil's Canyon. One prospector claimed to have found an eighty-five-pound solid gold rock in one of the old Spanish mine shafts.

At the entrance to Devil's Canyon, there is a grove of trees, some of them very old. On several of these trees can be found the barely discernable evidence of ancient markings, among them an outline of what appears to be a turtle. The image of a turtle has long been recognized by researchers as a symbol used by the Spanish to denote the existence of gold or silver nearby. Most often, the head of the turtle would be pointed in the direction of a mine or cache.

Farther up the canyon is another turtle symbol, this one far more mysterious. It consists of a giant outline of a turtle on the ground, one that was constructed using a total of one hundred and fifty-two stones. The head of the turtle was pointing to a portion of the northwest wall of the canyon. Some have claimed that the turtle was oriented toward the location of one of the old Spanish mines. Unfortunately, this image was subsequently destroyed during the construction of a stock pond in the canyon.

One old Indian legend claims that the canyon is haunted by the devil himself and that he guards the cache of gold the Indians concealed in one cliff. The legend also says that a layer of human skeletons covers the gold. In 1967, a youth was hunting rabbits in Devil's Canyon when he discovered a newly exposed opening in one of the canyon walls. The area had been subjected to heavy rains the previous week and several hundred pounds of rock and debris had been washed away, exposing the cave beyond. Peering into the opening, the boy saw several skeletons. Believing he had come upon a long-forgotten burial chamber, the youth did not investigate any further. He told no one of his experience until several years later. On hearing the story, a group of men familiar with the tales and legends of the Spanish and Mexican gold mining activities in Devil's Canyon traveled to the location in an attempt to locate the chamber and retrieve the gold. Though they spent several days searching for the old mines, they were unsuccessful.

Today, Devil's Canyon is part of Quartz Mountain State Park. The area is regularly visited by hikers and rock collectors. Some come to the canyon to search for evidence of the old Spanish and Mexican mines. If anyone has found the large cache of gold, they have not revealed it.

24

THE INCREDIBLE JOURNEY
OF THE CONFEDERATE TREASURY

The end of the Confederate States of America occurred during the spring of 1865. The South had suffered staggering defeats, leadership was in disarray, and the treasury did not contain enough money to continue the support of the war effort. The last official meeting of the leaders of the would-be nation was held in April at Abbeville, South Carolina, as President Jefferson Davis and his cabinet fled approaching Union forces.

The Confederate treasury, though depleted, was still a significant store of gold and silver coinage. Among the items debated by the Southern leaders was the fate of what remained of this money. Some researchers believe the decision makers decided to move the store of wealth in order to protect it from the Northern invaders. Others of a more cynical nature express confidence in the notion that the leaders wanted the gold and silver transported someplace where they might more easily get their hands on it following the Yankee victory

When General Robert E. Lee told President Davis that General Ulysses S. Grant's forces had penetrated the Confederate lines at Petersburg and that Richmond was about to be taken, Davis ordered an evacuation of the region. In the process, he placed the responsibility of moving the treasury to a new location with Captain William H. Parker.

Parker was an officer in the Confederate Navy with a stellar record. He took his new assignment seriously. On the afternoon of April 2, 1865, Parker, enlisting the help of sixty midshipmen from a training vessel anchored on the James River, loaded the entire wealth of the Confederate treasury into a boxcar. This was to be the first of many transfers to take place over the next few days. Around midnight, the train departed Richmond bearing, according to most experts, an estimated one million dollars. Others have suggested the amount was as high as thirty million dollars, but there exists little evidence to support such a claim.

By the time the train reached Danville, Parker received additional orders to move the treasure on to Charlotte, North Carolina, and store it in the abandoned U.S. Mint located there. No sooner was this done than Parker learned General George Stoneman's cavalry was headed in that direction and that the general might be interested in the treasure.

Parker ordered the treasure removed from the mint, packed into barrels with sacks of coffee, flour, and sugar, and reloaded onto the train. No sooner had this been accomplished than Parker was provided information that the railroad was out of service beyond Charlotte. He hurriedly transferred the containers from the train onto wagons.

While in the process of loading the treasure, Parker learned that Varina Davis, the wife of the Confederate president, was living in Charlotte with her children. Parker located her and persuaded her to travel south with him under military escort before the Union soldiers arrived.

On April 16, Parker's detachment arrived at Newberry, South Carolina. The trains were running, so the captain had the treasure-filled barrels and sacks loaded into another boxcar and continued toward Abbeville.

When the detachment reached Abbeville, Mrs. Davis decided to leave the train and remain with some friends who lived nearby. While Mrs. Davis seemed unconcerned, Parker was ill at ease with the arrangement. Convinced, however, that the Union cavalry was in pursuit of him and the treasure, he felt it necessary to abandon the area immediately. He decided to travel on to Washington, Georgia, a few miles across the Savannah River to the southwest. Since the train did not go in that direction, Parker once again had the treasure removed from the boxcar and loaded onto wagons. After bidding farewell to Mrs. Davis, he crossed the river into Georgia.

This part of Georgia had not suffered as much from Union raiding as had the rest of the state. Parker was confident he could locate a sizeable military unit here that could take over the responsibility for the gold and silver he was transporting. The captain was growing anxious to be rid of the burden of the entire wealth of the Confederate nation.

On arriving at Washington, Parker learned that a command of two hundred Confederate soldiers was holding Augusta fifty miles to the southeast. Running low on certain provisions, Parker traded flour and coffee to Washington residents for eggs, milk, and chickens. He then had his men load the treasure once more in a railroad car. Then he ordered the train to Augusta.

At Augusta, the frustrated Parker discovered that it was not as easy to reassign the treasure as he had hoped. The officers there informed him that the war was over and that they were merely awaiting the arrival of the Union troops to arrange for an orderly surrender of the town, receive their pay, and go home. Possession of the Confederate treasury, they explained to him, would complicate matters and they wanted nothing to do with it. One of the leaders even advised Parker to return the treasure to the now civilian leaders of the Confederate government who, at that very moment, were fleeing from Union soldiers across the Savannah River into Georgia. Among those in flight was Jefferson Davis himself.

Mistakenly, Parker decided Abbeville would be the likeliest place to locate Davis so he could ask him what to do with the treasure. He was convinced that Davis knew his wife was there and would try to find her. The fastest route to Abbeville was back through Washington, so Parker ordered the train to return. There, the now monotonous task of transferring the gold and silver back into wagons was once again completed and the journey to Abbeville was under way.

Less than one hour out of Washington, Parker, much to his surprise and chagrin, encountered Mrs. Davis and her children fleeing Abbeville with a small cavalry escort. She informed Parker she had not seen her husband and had no idea where he might be.

On April 28, Parker and his command finally arrived at Abbeville, unloaded the wealth from the wagons, stored it in an empty warehouse just outside of town and placed a heavy guard around it. That evening as he was dining, Parker received word from one of his scouts that a large contingent of Union forces was a few miles north of the town and would arrive soon. Panicked, Parker ordered his men to reload the treasure onto a railroad car. He then ordered the engineer to prepare to depart, but before the train could be started, several hundred soldiers appeared at the north end of the town, all riding straight toward the train.

Fortunately for the harried Parker, the soldiers turned out to be a Confederate company escorting President Davis and what was left of his cabinet. Parker met with Davis and related his misadventures with the treasury. To his great relief, Davis ordered the responsibility for the gold and silver transferred to the acting Secretary of the Treasury, John H. Reagan. Almost as quickly, Reagan shifted the responsibility to John C. Breckenridge, the Secretary of War. Breckenridge, not thrilled with this new and heavy burden, passed it on to General Basil Duke. Duke did not care for the responsibility either, but he had no one to pass it on to. Duke assumed the assignment with his customary dignity and rigid military bearing.

Duke was one of the few remaining Confederate generals and his command was a motley assortment of nearly one thousand poorly armed and equipped volunteers who wanted nothing more than to go home. They were deserting in droves. Once the soldiers learned the war was over, several at a time would slip away and return to their farms and homes throughout the now devastated South.

Close to midnight on May 2nd, General Duke urgently ordered the gold and silver transferred once again from the boxcar to wagons. Duke had learned earlier in the evening that Union patrols were thick in the area, and he felt he would be lucky to be able to transport the treasury farther south and away from the advancing Yankees. Duke believed that Union officials were now aware that the treasure was in the area and would attempt to seize it. With his remaining force of troops, Duke moved the treasure out of Abbeville during the dark of night. Jefferson Davis and his remaining cabinet, grateful for the escort, rode along. Several of the troops stayed far to the rear of the column keeping an eye out for pursuit, and a dozen more rode along the flanks, prepared to ward off an attack by Yankees.

During a rest stop around midmorning of the following day, Duke promised his soldiers that when they reached Washington they would be paid in gold coins from the treasury they were escorting. Knowing the war was over and anxious to be on their way, the troops clamored for payment on the spot. The soldiers were also concerned that Union troops might suddenly appear and seize the money before they could get what they were due. For the rest of the day, Duke and a paymaster counted out thirty-two dollars to each soldier in the command.

This done, the wagons were escorted across the Savannah River toward Washington, Georgia. Every few minutes, Duke received word from scouts that the Yankee soldiers were only minutes away from attacking his column. At the first opportunity, the general ordered his command to leave the trail and take refuge in a large farmhouse belonging to a man named Moss. The barrels and sacks of gold and silver were unloaded from the wagons and stacked in the farmhouse kitchen. Duke then stationed his men at strategic points around the farmhouse and told them to prepare for a Yankee attack on the traveling treasury The attack never materialized.

The Confederates spent the night at the farm. Very few of them were able to sleep since they were anticipating trouble at any moment. When scouts reported the next morning that no Yankees were in sight, Duke ordered the gold and silver loaded back onto the wagons. It was carried into Washington without incident.

At Washington, Duke turned the treasury over to Captain Micajah Clark. Earlier that day Jefferson, in his last official duty as President of the Confederacy, appointed Clark as the official treasurer of the Confederate States of America. Following this, Davis, along with his wife and children, fled deeper into the South. They were captured six days later.

Treasurer Clark decided that his first obligation in his new position was to count the money. According to the Treasury record, the exact amount was $288,000.90. It was, in truth, considerably less that what Parker had left Richmond with. Through the succeeding years, there had been a great deal of speculation as to what happened to the rest of the money. Thirty years later, Parker wrote an account of his adventures with the treasury and suggested that Captain Clark may have submitted a false accounting of what was turned over to him and kept the difference.

A significant number of researchers are convinced that Jefferson Davis himself appropriated much of the wealth before turning it over to Clark and then fled with it. They further speculated that Davis had buried portions of it at several different locations along the road before being apprehended. In any event, Clark paid off a few more of the soldiers out of the remaining funds and had the rest packed into kegs and wooden boxes.

On May 14, two officials representing a Virginia bank arrived in Washington with a federal order for the total amount of the treasury. The bank apparently held a claim on the wealth, and the two men were commissioned to secure it and return it to Richmond.

Following the military order to the letter, Clark turned what remained of the treasury over to the two bank representatives who, in turn, loaded it onto wagons and, under the protection of a military escort of some forty soldiers, departed for Richmond.

Most of the soldiers in the escort were young. And very few of them had seen any action during the war. For that reason, the two bank representatives were nervous throughout the trip. Soon after the column left Washington, a scout reported that it was being followed by a gang of outlaws made up of discharged Confederate soldiers and local toughs. The soldiers comprising the escort were ordered to take extra precautions as the small wagon train lumbered toward the Savannah River.

Travel was slow, and on the afternoon of May 22nd the party arrived at the front yard of the home of the Reverend Dionysius Chennault, only twelve miles out of Washington. The wagons were pulled into a large horse corral and drawn into a tight defensive circle. The guard was doubled and posted about the corral that night while the rest of the command tried to sleep.

At midnight the outlaws struck. Firing only a few shots, they surprised the inexperienced federal guards who quickly surrendered. The guards were tied up, and the remaining soldiers, who awakened at the first sound of shooting, were held at gunpoint by a handful of the outlaws. The leaders of the gang smashed open the boxes and kegs containing the gold and silver coins and stuffed their saddlebags full of the booty. Thousands of dollars' worth of coins were spilled onto the ground as the rest of the greedy outlaws surged forward and filled their pockets. Finally, carrying all they could hold, the outlaws mounted up and rode away on horses barely able to carry the combined weight of riders and loot. One of Reverend Chennault's daughters estimated that well over one hundred thousand dollars' worth of gold and silver coin was recovered from the ground the following morning.

The outlaws rode northwest to the bank of the Savannah River. On learning that they were being pursued by both Confederate soldiers as well as local law enforcement personnel, they hastily dug a pit and buried all of the wealth in a common cache. They intended to escape pursuit and return for it another time. They set up camp for the night, intending to depart in the morning. A company of soldiers encountered the bandits at dawn and killed every one of them.

What today is estimated to be worth well over one million dollars in Confederate gold and silver coins is still buried in the ground somewhere on the south bank of the Savannah River and just off the trail.

Members of the Chennault family gathered up the fortune in coins that had spilled onto the ground during the robbery. Placing the gold and silver into kitchen pots and wooden crates, they buried it in a shallow hole adjacent to a nearby tributary of the Savannah River. Though they waited for a significant amount of time, no representatives of either the Union or Confederate governments ever returned to the Chennault farm to claim any of the treasure.

The reverend cautioned his family members not to dig up any of the treasure until such time as the passions of the war died down and it would be safe to do so. Researchers have determined that the Chennault cache was never retrieved and still lies buried somewhere on the old farm. Over the years, a number of people have arrived at the farm to undertake a search for this rich portion of the Confederate treasury, but with no success.

In recent years, the state-of-the-art technology associated with metal detectors has improved to the point that a number of professional treasure hunters once again began developing plans to make additional attempts at recovering the Chennault farm treasure. They are disappointed to learn, however, that the small tributary near where the gold and silver were cached has been inundated by the waters of Clarks Hill Lake. According to the U.S. Army Corps of Engineers, the Chennault portion of the Confederate treasure lies beneath thirty feet of water today.

A WORD ABOUT SOURCES

I have been searching for and accumulating research and information on America's lost mines and buried treasures for close to six decades. During that time I have read and examined thousands of articles, documents, journals, diaries, maps, and books. To list all of the pertinent resources employed in the writing of this book would require almost as many pages. Should anyone be interested in pursuing their own research on some of the subjects treated in this book in greater depth, I recommend a simple Internet search.

In addition, and perhaps just as important, I have been involved in hundreds of interviews, conversations, discussions, and debates with other treasure hunters, professional and amateur, who have invested significant portions of their lives and finances over the decades in studying about and searching for many of the lost treasures described in this book. For these opportunities I am grateful, and the sharing of their knowledge and experience has contributed mightily to my store of information.

Finally, when it comes to research, nothing beats personal experience. In the course of my more than five decades as a professional treasure hunter, I have had the opportunity and pleasure to be involved with expeditions in search of most of the treasures described in this book. Sometimes I came away with important and valuable discoveries, sometimes not. Invariably I came away with knowledge and information to be filed away for the next quest. And I always experienced an adventure. After seven decades of living for the quest, I no longer get into the field as often as I would like. I suggest that it's time a new generation undertake the hunt. May you have as much success as I did.

ABOUT THE AUTHOR

W.C. Jameson is the award-winning author of more than eighty books. He is the bestselling treasure author in the United States and his prominence as a professional fortune hunter has led to stints as a consultant for the *Unsolved Mysteries* television show and the Travel Channel. He served as an advisor for the film *National Treasure* starring Nicolas Cage and appears in an interview on the DVD. His book *Treasure Hunter: Caches, Curses, and Deadly Confrontations* was named Best Book of the Year (2011) by Indie Reader. In 2013 he was inducted into the Professional Treasure Hunters Hall of Fame.

Jameson has written the soundtracks for two PBS documentaries and one feature film. His music has been heard on NPR and he wrote and performed in the musical *Whatever Happened to the Outlaw, Jesse James?* Jameson has acted in five films and has been interviewed on the History Channel, the Travel Channel, PBS, and *Nightline*. When not working on a book, he tours the country as a speaker, conducting writing workshops, and performing his music at folk festivals, concerts, roadhouses, and on television. He lives in Llano, Texas.